THE TRUTH WILL
SET YOU FREE

THE TRUTH WILL SET YOU FREE

*Commemorating
the 50th Anniversary of the Death
of Pope Pius XII*

Margherita Marchione

PAULIST PRESS
New York ● Mahwah, NJ

The author graciously acknowledges the charitable contribution given by Ann Petrocelli and the Petrocelli Foundation in memory of its founder, Anthony Petrocelli.

Jacket design by Sharyn Banks
Book design by John Eagleson

Library of Congress Cataloging-in-Publication Data

Marchione, Margherita.
    The truth will set you free : commemorating the fiftieth anniversary of the death of Pope Pius XII / Margherita Marchione.
        p. cm.
    Includes bibliographical references (p.   ) and index.
    ISBN 978-0-8091-0565-6 (alk. paper)
    1. Pius XII, Pope, 1876–1958. 2. Canonization. 3. Pius XII, Pope, 1876–1958 – Relations with Jews. 4. Holocaust, Jewish (1939–1945) 5. Judaism – Relations – Catholic Church. 6. Catholic Church – Relations – Judaism. 7. Christianity and antisemitism – History – 20th century. 8. World War, 1939–1945 – Religious aspects – Catholic Church. 9. National socialism and religion. I. Title.
    BX1378.M285 2008
    282.092 – dc22

                                                              2008025286

Published by Paulist Press
997 Macarthur Boulevard
Mahwah, New Jersey 07430

www.paulistpress.com

Printed and bound in the
United States of America

To His Holiness, Pope Benedict XVI,

a leading theologian and worthy successor of St. Peter

Contents

Preface

What should a reader look forward to in *The Truth Will Set You Free*? To finding a book written by a witness who has been untiringly committed to telling the truth about Pius in spite of a massive, clever, five-decades-long campaign of misinformation aimed at disgracing the wartime pope. Here is a cross-section of some of the basic information and insights the book offers:

+ Cardinal Tarcisio Bertone's foreword is the most revealing statement yet publicly issued by a high Vatican authority on "the Pope Pius controversy." It implicitly casts a great deal of light on the present pontificate's thinking about the campaign against Pius and the church. It also expresses appreciation for the author's twelve years of scholarly work on Pius.

+ The introduction powerfully re-creates the atmosphere of mourning and veneration that filled Rome and the high regard much of the world expressed at the time of Pius's funeral in 1958.

+ The book issues a challenge to those who call themselves Catholic to learn the truth about Pius and to speak out courageously. This appeal is especially aimed at Catholic educators — from elementary schools to universities — who have joined those peddling falsehoods and half-truths about Pius or have been co-opted to join the conspiracy of silence against him.

+ Sister Margherita Marchione takes on the sacrosanct professors of history advising Yad Vashem, the National Holocaust Museum in Jerusalem, for displaying inaccurate and insulting depictions of Pius.

+ The volume has several comments on and tributes to the author's pioneering work. One of the most telling is Cardinal Bertone's: "I recently made it known that in October 1943, Pope Pius sent out secret instructions to Catholic institutions informing them of their duty to shelter Jews from the Nazis. This news made headlines in Europe, but to those who have read any of Sister Margherita Marchione's books, it came as no surprise. She has interviewed literally dozens of witnesses who had firsthand knowledge of this and other similar instructions from the Pope."

+ Ronald Rychlak, law professor and author of two of the best books yet published on Pius, concludes that her "contributions to the Catholic Church are inestimable." He describes her as having "an uncanny knack of recognizing important evidence, verifying it, and recording it for prosperity. This has put her way ahead of most other researchers into this topic." He adds that in October 2007, at St. John's University in New York, she was "recognized by the Society of Catholic Social Scientists" and awarded "the Blessed Frederic Ozanam Award for Catholic Social Action."

+ Gary Krupp, Jewish founder and president of the ecumenical Pave the Way Foundation, issues his own challenge concerning the accuracy of her work: "I challenge any legitimate historic entity to prove any of the well-researched documented statements to be false." What the book does not reveal is that Krupp is now making a documentary video based to a large extent on witnesses uncovered by the author. His plan is to first show the video to a Jewish audience in Rome.

♦ The book coverage of the valuable scholarship of Jewish defenders ranges from Michael Tagliacozzo in 1963 to Sir Martin Gilbert in 2003. It also records how the Jewish press worldwide praised Pius's help for Jews throughout Hitler's reign of terror and expressed gratitude for saving hundreds of thousands of Jews. But in the last thirty years the same papers have repeated insupportable accusations about Pius's supposed "silence," while influential organizations like the Anti-Defamation League and World Jewish Congress have been in the forefront of efforts to block his beatification — based on those same inaccurate charges.

♦ Above all, this book deals with eyewitnesses and moral judgments, and calling the readers' attention to those who have failed to heed the testimony of witnesses and been unable to judge Pius fairly.

It might now be useful to add a few additional comments on the author's own sense of history as well as reflections on the incapacity of certain historians to comprehend a spiritual figure like Eugenio Pacelli.

As a historian, Sister Marchione is primarily interested in witnesses and singularly impatient with flawed interpreters of documents. She believes that those who allege Pius failed Jews who were being hunted down by Hitler's Gestapo have failed to examine carefully all the available evidence, and then, when the errors of their interpretations are pointed out, they shift to charging that the Vatican hasn't yet opened all its archives.

In her seven previous books on Pius, the author has told the world both how wrong his critics were and how wisely and faithfully he carried out his vows to shepherd the world according to the example of Jesus Christ.

Since 1963 there has been a heated dispute between defenders and accusers. But in recent years every relevant piece of new evidence — mainly from the recently released Pius XI documents — has reaffirmed Pacelli's opposition to Hitler and his defense of Jews, along with his wisdom and courage.

Reviewers over the last eleven years have pointed to her work as "uncompromising," "honest," "totally committed to the truth," "feisty," or even "combative." She is exceptional in that she practices full disclosure, hiding nothing, telling exactly where she's coming from and why. She is greatly disturbed by those who repeat the same old disproved charges against Pius — like he was "silent," or "indifferent," or "unconcerned about Jews."

This present volume underlines her interest in finding eyewitnesses who have been forgotten or ignored. Its overall thrust comes from the fact that many historians have been incapable of countering the dreadful effect of Rolf Hochhuth's cleverly presented smear that Pius was cold, silent, indifferent, and virtually a hangman for Jews. Instead of his being thrown out of the court of public opinion as frivolous, both Catholics and anti-Catholics accepted this Goebbels-style lie. Why?

The great historical theorist Robin Collingwood described the ideal state of mind for a historian to be one who takes pleasure in doubt, as "intelligent skepticism." From such a viewpoint no historic ethical or moral disagreement is ever likely to be settled permanently. For him historic argumentation is a heady game (like chess) played with evidence. Those in possession of the most and best evidence will win the game, with the possibility always existing that a new piece of evidence may force us to revise our position. The game goes on until there appears to be no more new evidence, although it is theoretically possible that sometimes new evidence will turn up — like the DNA evidence that led to a reappraisal of the life of Thomas Jefferson.

Marchione admires objectivity but makes no claim to be an impartial historian. What she knows about Pius, having studied him for over a decade, convinces her that no new document will appear to prove Pius was a time-serving scoundrel in papal robes indifferent to the fate of any of Hitler's victims. She, like all of Pius's defenders, is convinced of three things: that a colossal fraud was carried out against Pius XII by Rolf Hochhuth's libelous *The Deputy* (1963), that a generation was brainwashed by those lies, among them some respected historians, and that sound patient scholarship over the last forty years has reputed every charge made by Hochhuth and those following his lead.

Some of the author's detractors would object that she makes moral appraisals that no historian should make. But no one can write intelligently on Pius without entering a world where moral and religious judgments are at the heart of every word uttered and action taken. One who cannot comprehend and weigh Pius's faith is prevented from reaching correct and just conclusions because they lack sufficient comprehension of Pius's world.

Owen Chadwick, generally regarded as Britain's leading twentieth-century church historian, writes in *Catholicism and History*: "Wherever the historian . . . needs to enter the realm of moral judgment, the nature of his own moral stance begins to matter. Those who say that historians never enter the realm of judgment live in dreams. Man being what he is, moral judgment is inseparable from any other form of judgment about people and their effect upon their world. It should play little or no part in historical synthesis. But it can never be wholly absent from the historian's stance. You can exclude moral judgment only by restricting yourself to a heap of facts — that is, by not writing history."

At the center of the vilification of Pius is the absence of any interest in or trust in his quest for holiness. His detractors always seek to see him mainly as a political figure. They resist any serious consideration of what it meant that he lived a life of prayer and devotion.

In this book Sister Margherita is both a witness and historian. She battles with Pius's critics and at the same time is more interested in living witnesses than archival documents and those who would depend solely on those documents. Of course she has the utmost respect for documents, but her major contribution is her contact with those who have firsthand, eyewitness knowledge. Thus her long article on a historian she greatly admires, Michael Tagliacozzo, who lived through the Roman roundup of 1943. She sees the protracted "Pius XII controversy" not as coming from equally well-informed scholars holding equally valid views of Pius, but as more of a vendetta carried out by a small number of agenda-driven partisans eager to satisfy the scandal-famished media. Too often their judgment of Pius's moral conduct is indistinguishable from that of bigots out to blacken the pope's reputation and malign the Catholic Church by bearing false witness against both.

Unmentioned in this book is the fact that Sister has done fundamental research on miracles attributed to Pius. Some years ago she located in the United States and Canada two people who claimed to have been miraculously cured by Pius's intercession. She reported these cases to the Congregation for the Causes of Saints. As the years passed those claiming cures died. In the most promising of these cases, in Delaware, an extensive examination had been carried out. But she found that all the documentation disappeared when the original pastor retired and a new one took over.

Michael O'Carroll, author of one of the best books written on Pius (*Pius XII: Greatness Dishonoured*, 1980), calls Hochhuth's broadside "the greatest literary lie of modern times" and comments: "A whole generation of intellectuals were caught, and intellectuals do not easily admit their error. . . . The world needs intellectuals. But it needs them free of illusions about themselves, . . . free to admit, as in the present instance, when they have been well and thoroughly fooled."

Sister Marchione in this book is trying to make sure that no one else will be fooled by Hochhuth's falsehoods.

Fiftieth anniversaries of holy men and women and the most remarkable pontiffs in the history of the church are customarily golden occasions greeted with pealing bells, prayers of gratitude, speeches filled with joyous memories, and new volumes of glowing testimony. It is becoming more evident that Benedict XVI and serious Catholics in Spain, the United States, and elsewhere are going to see that the jubilee year of Pius's death will be a time of joy and serious attention to this pontiff's great contribution to the church.

ROBERT MOYNIHAN, PH.D.
Editor, *Inside the Vatican*

Foreword

For over a decade, Sister Margherita Marchione's books on Pope Pius XII have been available both in English and in Italian. Her present book, *The Truth Will Set You Free*, in commemoration of the fiftieth anniversary of the death of Pope Pius XII, culminates her efforts.

In the past I have defended Pius XII, the 262nd successor of St. Peter. Recently I have also expressed my interest in the controversy surrounding this twentieth-century pope.

On January 25, 2007, during the presentation in Rome of the Italian translation of his book *The Righteous*, Jewish historian Sir Martin Gilbert defined as "false" the accusations about Pius XII during the Shoah and spoke about the commendable actions of the pontiff and of the Catholic Church, which in league with the efforts of other rescuers saved Jewish lives.

It sufficed to mention Don Aldo Brunacci, who testified that his bishop, Giuseppe Placido Nicolini, received a letter from Pius XII instructing him to protect persecuted Jews in Assisi. The testimony of Emilio Viterbi, a Jewish refugee in Assisi, also confirms Pius XII's involvement in the rescue of Jews by religious institutes. He referred to the guidance of Bishop Nicolini, "who with the greatest love and highest zeal had thus followed the philanthropic will of the Holy Father."

During the conference, I strongly defended Pope Pius XII against critics who charge that the pontiff failed to protect

Jews during the Holocaust. With reference to the church's intervention, I pointed out: "It is clear that Pope Pacelli was not about silence but about intelligent and strategic speaking, as demonstrated in the 1942 Christmas radio message, which infuriated Hitler. The proofs are in the Vatican archives.... Research done by independent historians confirm that Pope Pius XII took extraordinary steps to save Jewish lives."

Again, on April 17, 2007, I spoke about the subject, recalling the circular letter of the secretary of state, dated October 25, 1943, with Pius XII's initials, giving orders to the religious institutes and the catacombs to save as many Jews as possible. Those who follow the news out of Rome know that recently I publicly revealed that in October 1943 Pope Pius sent out secret instructions to Catholic institutions informing them of their duty to shelter Jews from the Nazis. This news made headlines in Europe, but to those who have read any of Sister Margherita Marchione's books, this was no surprise. She has interviewed literally dozens of witnesses who had firsthand knowledge of this and other similar instructions from the pope.

My words on June 5, 2007, give testimony to my belief that Pius XII is worthy of beatification. I carefully analyzed the "Black Legend." I gave testimony to a man of the church, who by his personal holiness shines as a luminous witness of the Catholic priesthood and of the papacy. After reading books by Pierre Blet, Margherita Marchione, Andrea Tornielli, and countless other authors, I can only repeat my convictions that with his many encyclicals Pope Pius XII established doctrinal norms, gave impetus to missionary activity, and affirmed women's rights to action even in the political and judiciary fields.

One cannot speak of Pius XII's silence. He spoke in the course of his radio messages, and so it is completely out of place to speak of his "silences." A well-documented article entitled "Il Silenzio di Pio XII: alle origini della leggenda nera" (The Silence of Pius XII: At the Origins of the Black Legend), by Professor Gian Maria Vian (editor of *L'Osservatore Romano*) was published in 2004 in the prestigious journal *Archivum Historiae Pontificiae*.

According to Vian, the first writer to ask about the "Silences of Pius XII" was French Catholic philosopher Emmanuel Mounier in 1939, just a few weeks after the election of the supreme pontiff. The article, of Soviet and Communist origin, was in relation to Italian aggression in Albania. This bitter polemic was continued by Rolf Hochhuth, author of *The Deputy*. Both contributed to the creation of the "Black Legend" against Pius XII.

Because of his prudent approach, Pius XII was able to protect Jews and other refugees. One must also consider that many times during World War II, the Fascist government made sure that Vatican Radio "did not have the requisite electricity" to make the pontiff's voice heard; that many times there was "a scarcity of paper" to reproduce his thoughts and uncomfortable teachings against Nazism and Fascism; that many times some "accident" caused issues of *L'Osservatore Romano*, which carried clarifications, updates, political notes, etc., to be lost or destroyed.

For the past decade, Sister Margherita Marchione has gathered documents that prove outrageous the misrepresentations about Pope Pius XII's so-called "silence" and "anti-Semitism." With her book *Did Pope Pius XII Help the Jews?* (2007), she has proven that Pius XII was not silent, nor was he anti-Semitic. He was prudent. Had he taken a more public stand, he would have endangered the lives of thousands of Jews who, at his direction, were hidden in 155 convents and monasteries in Rome alone.

As author of this new book, she reminds us that it was Pope Pius XII who authorized false baptismal certificates to save Jewish lives. He also provided visas for Jews to enter other countries and ordered the superiors of convents and monasteries to open their doors and hide Jews and other victims of the Nazis and the Fascists. Angelo Roncalli (the future Pope John XXIII), who also distributed many certificates, stated that all he was doing was following the pope's directives. Over fifty years have passed since the apostolic nuncio in Istanbul wrote in his *Diary* about an audience with Pope Pius XII on October 10, 1941, declaring that the pope's statements were "prudent."

On June 2, 1943, when Pius XII spoke of the Jewish people he stated: "The rulers of nations must not forget that he who 'carries the sword' — to use the language of Sacred Scripture — cannot decide the life and death of men except in accord with the law of God, from whom all authority comes.... You cannot expect us here to recount point for point all that we have tried to procure and accomplish to mitigate their sufferings, to better their moral and juridical condition, to safeguard their inalienable religious rights, to bring help in their sufferings and necessities. Every word to this end that we addressed to the competent authorities as well as each of our public allusions had to be weighed and measured by us in the very interest of those who were suffering, so that we should not unwittingly make their situation more grave and unbearable." Here then, in the middle of 1943, Pope Pius XII revealed the reason for the prudence with which he conducted himself in public denouncements, "in the very interest of those who were suffering."

Pius XII's neutrality saved not only Europeans but other prisoners as well. He knew that the fate of millions depended on his every word. Robert Kempner, a Jewish lawyer and public official at the Nuremberg trials, wrote in 1964: "Any propagandistic position that the church would have taken against Hitler's government would have not only provoked suicide, but it would have hastened the execution of still more Jews and priests."

In conclusion, I would like to thank those who, like Sister Margherita Marchione, have contributed to a better understanding of the luminous apostolic action of the figure of this Servant of God, Pius XII. How profoundly unjust it is to judge the work of Pius XII during the war with the veil of prejudice, forgetting not only the historical context but also the enormous work of charity that the pope promoted, opening the doors of seminaries and religious institutes, welcoming refugees and persecuted people, helping all who were in need. Directives given by Pope Pius XII on the radio, in the press, and through diplomatic channels were clear. In that tragic year of 1942 he told everyone: "Action, not lamentation, is the precept of the hour."

CARDINAL TARCISIO BERTONE

Introduction

As we commemorate the fiftieth anniversary of the death of Pope Pius XII on October 9, 1958, we are also joined by our Jewish brethren who celebrate Yom Kippur. On the eve of this most sacred Hebrew holy day, Jews gather in synagogues to begin their fast and return the following morning to continue praying for forgiveness. Hopefully, on this day, Jews and Catholics will understand one another and together pray for forgiveness. Catholics and Jews can no longer continue to condone statements by those who defame Pope Pius XII, ignore and distort the facts, or limit themselves to the opinion of prejudiced writers.

In fact, ever since the death of Pope Pius XII in 1958, every pope from John XXIII to Benedict XVI has noted his sanctity. In his first Christmas message, John XXIII said his predecessor was worthy of canonization and called him, "Doctor Optimus, Ecclesiae Sanctae Lumen, Divinae Legis Amatur" (supreme doctor, light of holy mother church, lover of the divine law).

In an effort to explain why the investigation of Pope Pius XII's beatification has been delayed, Andrea Tornielli reported that the Vatican did not doubt the holiness of Pope Pius XII, but was concerned about the effects his beatification would have. Could acknowledgment of his sanctity adversely affect relations with Jews and the state of Israel? Supporters of the wartime pope, who reigned from 1939 to 1958, consider the delay unnecessary. Or is the delay because the U.S.-based Anti-Defamation League and other Jewish groups have asked that the canonization inquiry be suspended until all Vatican archives related to World War II are declassified?

Pius XII was a saintly pontiff who worked behind the scenes to help Jews throughout the continent. He ordered churches and convents in Rome to take in Jews after the Germans occupied the city in 1943. The Vatican holds that Pope Pius did not speak out more forcefully for fear of further Nazi reprisals that would worsen the position of both Catholics and Jews throughout Europe. Who can deny Pope Pius XII's "heroic virtues"?

Fifty years have passed and now Pope Benedict has commissioned a new committee to review old documents and examine new ones recently discovered in the Secretariat of State. No doubt they will help clarify, re-evaluate, and remove any doubts concerning Pope Pius XII's so-called "silence" during World War II. Hopefully, these documents, after being released to the competent Congregation and to the public domain during this fiftieth anniversary of his death, will help dispel the myth of "Hitler's Pope" and reaffirm his titles of "Defensor Civitatis" and "Pastor Angelicus."

Honoring Pope Pius XII on his death in 1958, Cardinal Richard Cushing stated: "Theologian, canonist, scholar, linguist, statesman, diplomat — all of these Pius XII was. For all of them he has been hailed and praised. But more than anything else he was a pastor, a good shepherd of souls, selflessly dedicated to the honest interests of the Church and to the greater glory of God."

Pope Pius XII was the object of unanimous admiration and gratitude. "The world," President Eisenhower declared, "is now poorer following the death of Pope Pius XII." And Golda

Meir, foreign secretary for the State of Israel, said: "Life in our time was enriched by a voice which expressed the great moral truths over the tumult of daily conflicts. We lament the loss of a great servant of peace."

Rabbi Joachim Prinz, national president of the American Jewish Congress, stated: "Among his many great contributions to mankind, the pontiff will be remembered wherever men of good will gather for his profound devotion to the cause of peace and for his earnest efforts in the rescue of thousands of victims of Nazi persecution, including many Jewish men, women and children."

When Pope Pius XII died on October 9, 1958, Jews everywhere praised him for his help and were among the first to express sorrow and gratitude for his solicitude in saving Jews during the Holocaust. In fact there were so many statements that the *New York Times* could list only the names of their authors. For example, in the issue for October 9, 1958: Bernard Baruch; Rabbi Theodore L. Adams, president of the Synagogue Council of America; Irving M. Engel, president of the American Jewish Committee, and Jacob Blaustein and Joseph M. Proshauer, honorary presidents; Dr. Israel Goldstein, chairman of the Western Hemisphere World Jewish Congress; Rabbi Alan Steinech, president of the New York Board of Rabbis; Mrs. Moise S. Cahn, president of the National Council of Jewish Women; Rabbi Jacob P. Rudin, president of the Central Conference of American Rabbis. In the October 10, 1958, issue: Rabbi Emanual Rockman, president of the Rabbinical Council of America, and Isaac H. Herzog. Among the tributes in the October 11, 1958, issue was one by the Jewish Labor Committee. All referred to the work the pope and the Vatican had done to save Jews during the Second World War.

On October 10, 1958, the *New York Times* reported that Leonard Bernstein began the performance of the New York Philharmonic the previous evening with a tribute by Harold C. Schonberg, and by Bernstein asking the audience to stand in silence for one minute, in tribute to Pius XII. Two days later, the *Times* reported the numerous memorial services for the late pope in the synagogues of New York City.

Ronald Threm, a young man from New Jersey, also honored Pius XII when he died. He gathered clippings from the most important American newspapers and carefully bound them in a book titled in gold lettering: *Death of Pope Pius XII.*

In a conversation with me, Father Antonio Furioli recalled the emotion experienced when Pius XII died. Everyone in his family loved him. Antonio was very young and cried with his mother and family. He stated: "Everyone was sad. For days my mother kept a candle lighted before an image of Pius XII and together we prayed and shed tears. It was a spontaneous and sincere tribute toward someone we felt was a family friend. I remember that I was inconsolable. This was my first experience with death, the first great sorrow of my life. Pius XII remained a model that inspired me to become a priest."

To capture the sentiments of the American public, it is interesting to note an editorial in the *Los Angeles Examiner* declaring that this "Fighter for Peace" was the "Pope of Peace": "It was God's will that the leader of the Roman Catholic Church through years of grave trial should be a man with beautifully sensitive hands, a face of compassionate wisdom, a frail body, and a voice of quiet and profound solace." Today, the hostile attacks by the media, characterizing Pius as a weak, cold church bureaucrat, insult the historical records that show him as an uncommonly good and saintly twentieth-century pope.

Pius XII gave hope and courage to millions during the war and saved more Jewish victims from the Nazis than any other individual or combination of individuals. Winning more admiration and praise from the faithful than any of his pontifical predecessors since the Reformation, he restored church prestige and provided all faiths of the world with extraordinary leadership. He was spontaneous, informal, and human. However, he was also very solemn, serious, formal, and not only commanded respect but, at times, fear and concern from those working with him. In his personal relations Pacelli was affectionate as he gently lifted young children and tenderly held babies in his arms. During papal audiences, he reached out to the faithful, to prisoners of war, the wounded and maimed.

Perhaps one can say that Pope Pius XII was the world's most powerful twentieth-century leader. He was a clear-minded realist with an all-encompassing sense of human existence. His search for peace was all-consuming, and his speeches and writings are a priceless heritage. His reputation, no matter how vilified, is praised and honored by Catholics and Jews.

As a member of the Religious Teachers Filippini, with close ties to the papal household and personal knowledge of the Pacelli family, I have written books and articles in English and in Italian telling the inspiring story of Eugenio Pacelli simply and faithfully.

To offset misunderstandings and to correct false reports, I have endeavored to contribute to the true history of modern Jewish-Catholic relations by recording the witness of Jews and Catholics and by reproducing Vatican documentary records. My scholarship in defense of Pope Pius XII challenges the careless innuendoes and unfounded accusations that have been leveled against his good name and reputation as a courageous and holy pastor of souls.

On the fiftieth anniversary of the death of Pius XII, we recall the outstanding contribution his life made to the world. I have been in the forefront of the battle to restore the reputation of this contribution of Pope Pius XII to its saintly rank. This selection of my writings and of others bears testimony to my passion for Truth.

One

Charges and Challenges

Only the Church stood squarely across the path of Hitler's campaign for suppressing the truth.
— Albert Einstein

Background History

Eugenio Pacelli's interest in equal rights for Jews dates back to the beginning of the twentieth century. On December 30, 1915, the American Jewish Committee appealed to Pope Benedict XV to use his moral influence and speak out against anti-Semitism. Within a few weeks (February 9, 1916), Vatican secretary of state Cardinal Pietro Gasparri signed a declaration prepared by Pacelli, which states: "The Catholic Church, faithful to its divine doctrine ... considers all men as brothers and teaches them to love one another ... [and] never ceases to inculcate among individuals, as well as among peoples, the observance of the principles of natural law and to condemn everything which violates them. This law must be observed and respected in the case of the children of Israel, as well as of all others.... "

Early in the crucial year of 1940 — when Axis victory seemed likely — Pius XII cooperated with President Franklin Roosevelt, attempting to persuade Mussolini not to join

Hitler's war. These efforts failed. In June of that year, Benito Mussolini joined Hitler in the war and escalated his own anti-Semitic policies (first introduced in 1938). News services in Italy were censored and reports about German atrocities labeled as propaganda. Still, in a wide array of languages, Vatican Radio broadcasted a description and denunciation of German policy in Poland. Later, Vatican Radio addressed the persecution of Jews, warning Catholics, "He who makes a distinction between Jews and other men is unfaithful to God and in conflict with God's commands."

The charge that Pius XII and the Catholic Church were silent as the Jews of Europe were murdered is compounded by the accusation that the church failed to live up to its moral and spiritual values.

Critics of Pius XII's "silence" claim that he never explicitly condemned the murder of the Jews and its perpetrators. His supporters maintain that his words, though measured, were nevertheless clearly understood as a condemnation of Nazi ideology and anti-Semitism. An examination of Vatican Radio broadcasts during 1940–42 shows that these programs consistently opposed any form of collaboration with Nazi ideology and stood for the sanctity of human life regardless of descent by informing its listeners about the persecution and murder of the Jews.

When Pius XII learned that thousands of Jews were being exterminated in the concentration camps, he asked Archbishop Francis Spellman of New York to verify these vicious crimes. He also immediately arranged for Diego von Bergen, the German ambassador to the Vatican, to meet with him and bitterly denounced the horrors taking place. In response to the Holy Father's tirade against the Nazis' cruelty, von Bergen menacingly stated: "I shall report your feelings to the Führer.

Do not be surprised if relations between the Third Reich and the Papacy are broken off."

Not only did the Vatican issue citizenship papers to Jews, but documents show that, at the direction of Pope Pius XII, visas were obtained for four hundred Jews to be accepted in Santo Domingo, and eight hundred Jews for travel to the United States. Furthermore, false baptismal papers were distributed everywhere by his representatives. No wonder there were threats throughout these years to sack the Vatican, kidnap the pope, and bring him to Germany.

The Nazis had solidified their power in the early 1930s, and ferocious retaliation had been the typical response to every Vatican protest. Tibor Baransky, a board member of the United States Holocaust Memorial Council and a Yad Vashem honoree, recalls that "Papal Nuncios helped the Jews. They got their orders straight from the pope." He recounted that, while working at the age of twenty-two as a special representative of Angelo Rotta, the papal nuncio in Hungary, he heard from Jewish leaders who asked the pope not to raise a public outcry over the Nazi atrocities — since it would likely only increase their ferocity. Working with Rotta, Baransky carried blank documents and forged protective passes and fake baptismal certificates to save as many Jewish lives as possible. When Nazis and their local sympathizers ignored these documents, Rotta sent Baransky to retrieve them.

In the private archives of Jay Pierrepont Moffat, who headed the U.S. State Department's European division before World War II, there is a 1939 report by Alfred Klieforth, then United States consul general in Cologne, Germany. Referring to the then cardinal Eugenio Pacelli, Klieforth reported that the cardinal "opposed unilaterally every compromise with National Socialism. He regarded Hitler not only as an untrustworthy scoundrel but as a fundamentally wicked person. He did not believe Hitler capable of moderation, in spite of appearances, and he fully supported the German bishops in their anti-Nazi stand."

In a four-page report to Ambassador Joseph Kennedy, father of President John F. Kennedy, Cardinal Pacelli made clear that the Nazi program struck at the fundamental principle of the freedom of the practice of religion and indicated the emergence of a Nazi culture war against the church.

The Nazi Roundup

Pius XII deserves the Yad Vashem title "Righteous Gentile." He did not close his eyes during the Nazi roundup of Roman Jews on October 16, 1943. No one expected the German military commander to send an SS force into the Roman quarter. They plundered the synagogue's library and sent its precious manuscripts to Munich. Nazi troops searched for Jews: men and women, young and old, entire families were captured and loaded into trucks for transportation to the Auschwitz concentration camp in Poland.

During an interview with Princess Enza Pignatelli Aragona Cortes, she explained how she rushed to the Vatican and personally alerted Pius XII in the early hours of the roundup. She reported that Pius XII was "furious" when he learned about it and immediately sent for Cardinal Luigi Maglione, Vatican secretary of state, who delivered the official papal protest to the German ambassador, Ernst von Weizsäcker. The protest expressed the pope's profound distress over the fact that, "under his very eyes," poor and innocent people should have to suffer simply because they were of a particular race and for no other reason. Weizsäcker, convinced that an intervention with Berlin would produce the opposite of the intended effect, assured Cardinal Maglione that he would do everything possible at the local level to cope with the threat to the Jews of Rome. He downplayed the papal reaction and convinced Berlin not to launch an attack on the Vatican. In the Nazi plan, 8,000 Roman Jews were marked for elimination. During the raid, 1,259 Jews were transported to a temporary detention center in the Italian Military College. After meticulous examination of identity documents and other papers of identification, 259 people were released the following day. The others were later transported to Rome's Tiburtina Station, where they were crowded into empty freight cars bound for Auschwitz.

According to the State of Israel Ministry of Justice, "The Trial of Adolf Eichmann: Record of Proceedings in the District Court of Jerusalem" (vol. 1, 83, Jerusalem, 1992), a report from Rome to Berlin, dated October 26, 1943, confirmed that the "Vatican has apparently for a long time been assisting many Jews escape." The British representative to the Holy See sent a secret telegram to the Foreign Office in which he reported: "As soon as he heard of the arrests of Jews in Rome, Cardinal Secretary of State sent for the German Ambassador and formulated some [sort] of protest." The result, according to British records, was that "large numbers" of the Jews were released.

In the *Jewish Chronicle* (London) of October 29, 1943, an editorial entitled "Jewish Hostages in Rome: Vatican Protests" stated: "The Vatican has made strong representations to the German government and the German High Command in Italy against the persecution of the Jews in Nazi occupied Italy." After the Vatican protest, the operation was immediately suspended.

Supporters and Critics

Expressions of gratitude on the part of Jewish chaplains and Holocaust survivors give witness to the assistance and compassion of the pope. In the January 2008 issue of *Inside the Vatican,* Sir Martin Gilbert was selected as one of the ten people who made a difference in the past year. The magazine regards him as a great historian and a model of integrity, "not only because he is a world-acclaimed historian, but especially because throughout his career he has been a fair-minded, conscientious collector of facts." In dealing with the church, the Vatican, and especially Pope Pius XII, Sir Martin Gilbert presents historical events without disdain and takes seriously "the Judeo-Christian ethic."

Recently Sir Martin Gilbert was interviewed by Andrea Tornielli for the Italian newspaper *Il Giornale:* "Priests and bishops saved Jews wherever they were threatened, including Poland, France, and Italy.... The Nazis recognized the fact that Pope Pius XII directed his representatives to save the persecuted Jews by opening the doors of Catholic institutions. They considered Pope Pius XII an enemy of Germany." The point Martin Gilbert made about the kidnapping of the pope was that it would have had disastrous consequences for Catholics throughout the area under German rule.

Gilbert stated that when the Gestapo came to Rome in 1943 to round up Jews, the Catholic Church, on the pope's direct authority, immediately dispersed as many Jews as they could. In his book *Never Again: The History of the Holocaust* (2000), Gilbert thanks the Vatican for what was done, even providing false passports and false baptismal certificates to save Jewish lives. In an editorial (1941), the *New York Times* praised the pope for having "put himself squarely against

Hitlerism." The pope explicitly condemned "the wickedness of Hitler" (October 15, 1940) and "the immoral principles of Nazism" (March 30, 1941).

Gilbert comments on the charge that Pius XII was "silent about Nazi murder" and states that this is a serious error of historical fact. He argues that it would have been highly irresponsible for the pope to have spoken in a provocative way. He writes about how the Nazis viciously accused Pius XII of being "the mouthpiece of the Jewish war criminals." True historians, according to Sir Martin Gilbert, acquire relevant facts, weigh carefully the surrounding circumstances, and do not impose personal preconceptions on the reader.

Within the last few years, there have been many books that deal with the controversy about Pius XII. Four authors who have defended Pius XII are Pierre Blet (*Pius XII and the Second World War*), Ronald Rychlak (*Hitler, the War and the Pope*), Ralph McInerny (*The Defamation of Pius XII*), and myself (*Pope Pius XII: Architect for Peace*). Other books take up Pius XII as part of a broad attack against Catholicism: Garry Wills (*Papal Sin*) and James Carroll (*Constantine's Sword*). Three authors unjustly vilify Pope Pius XII: John Cornwell (*Hitler's Pope: The Secret History of Pius XII*), Michael Phayer (*The Catholic Church and the Holocaust, 1930–1965*), and Susan Zuccotti (*Under His Very Windows: The Vatican and the Holocaust in Italy*). Unfortunately, the books by Cornwell, Phayer, and Zuccotti have received most of the attention.

John Cornwell contends that Pope Pius XII helped start World War I and World War II, betrayed German Catholics, and assisted in the Holocaust. Cornwell deals in rumors, half-truths, and misrepresentations.

Cornwell's alleged "findings" have been destroyed by competent scholars. An abundance of evidence exists that obliterates the myths about the "black legend" regarding Pius XII's wartime record. The controversy has now expanded into a direct attack against the pope, as well as against the entire Roman Catholic Church.

Pius XII addressed the dilemma of the extermination of the Jews in a communication to the Sacred College of Cardinals. He called attention to "the anxious entreaties of all those who, because of their nationality or their race are being subjected to overwhelming trials and, sometimes, through no fault of their own, are doomed to extermination.... Every word We address to the competent authority on this subject, and all Our public utterances, have to be carefully weighed and measured by Us in the interests of the victims themselves, lest, contrary to Our intentions, We make their situation worse and harder to bear.... The ameliorations apparently obtained do not match the scope of the Church's maternal solicitude on behalf of the particular groups that are suffering the most appalling fate. The Vicar of Christ, who asked no more than pity and a sincere return to elementary standards of justice and humanity, then found himself facing a door that no key could open" (June 2, 1943).

While it is difficult to repair the damage done by the controversial book *Hitler's Pope,* which was on the *New York Times* bestseller list for five weeks, we can rejoice to learn that the author has finally conceded he was mistaken with regard to Pius XII. John Cornwell claimed he wanted to vindicate the pope; instead, his book is an indictment of the pontiff's alleged collaboration with the Nazis. The author has since modified his views.

In a Features and Opinion article in the *Catholic Herald* (July 27, 2007), Britain's leading Catholic newspaper, Cornwell stated: "I've never accused Pius of being a Nazi....I would now argue, in the light of the debates and evidence following *Hitler's Pope,* that Pius XII had so little scope for action that it is impossible to judge the motives for his silence during the war while Rome was under the heel of Mussolini and later occupied by Germany.

"What the book is really about is the penalties you pay for having over-centralisation in the Church. And you can't tell what these penalties are, how weakened the Church is by centralisation, until the chips are down and there's a great struggle. A lot of people have misunderstood the book, and possibly it's my fault — the title could so easily be misunderstood.

"I've never accused him of being a wicked man, a Nazi or anything like that. The one thing I would say is that ethically if he did use political and diplomatic language and minced his words during the war, he had an obligation after the war when the pressures were off him to explain why he did it to those many people who were scandalised. And he never did." Not true! The documents prove that he did speak. (A more complete response to John Cornwell may be found in my book *Did Pope Pius XII Help the Jews?* [2007].)

Zuccotti's book, on the other hand, admits the truth about the role of the Catholic Church and then adds personal remarks that serve to blind the reader to historical truth. She also claims that there are no witnesses today who can testify that they, at the direction of Pius XII, helped save Jews.

The following document destroys Zuccotti's thesis that there is no evidence of a papal directive to church institutions to shelter Jews. It was written on September 26, 2000: "I, Sister Domenica Mitaritonna, declare under oath that during the period of the war 1942–1943, I was living at 16 Via Caboto, Rome, and assisted two or three Jewish families who sought refuge in our convent. They were welcomed with immense hospitality by the Superior who had been solicited by the Vatican to help them."

Zuccotti did not consult the nine hundred pages of sworn depositions for Pius XII's cause for beatification. These testimonials make it clear that he was not anti-Semitic, that he was not "silent." The charges claiming "silence," "moral culpability," or "anti-Semitism" can be refuted by anyone who examines evidence dispassionately. These charges form part of a much wider spectrum of political and ideological attacks on Christianity.

Susan Zuccotti's book claims that Pope Pius XII never instructed religious to protect Jews during the war. This statement is contradicted by the Chief Rabbi of Rome, Israel Zolli, who devoted an entire chapter in his 1954 memoirs, *Before the Dawn,* to the German occupation of Rome and praised the pope's leadership: "The Holy Father sent by hand a letter to the bishops instructing them to lift the enclosure from convents and monasteries, so that they could become a refuge for the Jews. I know of one convent where the Sisters slept in the basement, giving up their beds to Jewish refugees. In face of this charity, the fate of so many of the persecuted is especially tragic."

In the *New York Times Magazine* (February 4, 2001) historian Christopher Duggan continues the debate over Pope Pius XII and the Holocaust. Speaking of Zuccotti's book, Duggan writes: "This is a serious and well-researched book. . . . But is it good history? For all its scholarship, it feels driven by a remorseless desire to find wanting. Credit is given in places; but for the most part the text is a litany of phrases like 'it was not enough,' 'that was all,' 'it was very little,' 'lamentable,' 'he was wrong,' 'should have' — phrases that repeatedly raise questions about the author's intellectual, as well as moral, vantage point. Zuccotti condemns, but offers little new insight into why the Vatican and Pius acted as they did."

Finally, when Rolf Hochhuth's fictional play *The Deputy* (1963) unjustly condemned Pius XII, the Vatican archives were opened at the direction of Pope Paul VI, who engaged four Jesuit historians to study the documents. More than five thousand documents were published in twelve volumes. Historian Eamon Duffy stated that these volumes "decisively established the falsehood of Hochhuth's specific allegations."

The Challenge for Catholics and Jews

Today Pius XII is maligned and denigrated. Catholics must promote the truth about Pope Pius XII and comment in the media. We must defend him by offering incontestable evidence to obliterate the myths and lies that continue to be circulated by the media.

This "truth" must be taught in Catholic schools and religious education programs by including Holocaust education in the regular curriculum. Objectives should include promoting respect, freedom, and opportunity for all, regardless of nationality, religion, or race; explaining that Pope Pius XII was not silent during the war; teaching about the work of rescuers whose extraordinary acts of courage saved many Jews from death; emphasizing American Jewry's appreciation for his extraordinary accomplishments during the Holocaust;

and demonstrating that his humanitarianism was a new and
effective method of fighting anti-Semitism.

Documents show that in 1939, in a last-minute bid to avert
bloodshed, the pope called for a peace conference involving
Italy, France, England, Germany, and Poland. Pius XII's peace
plan was based upon the five points he first put forth in his
1939 Christmas speech. These proposals contained, among
other things, the defense of small nations, the right to life,
disarmament, some new kind of League of Nations, and a
plea for the moral principles of justice and love.

The 1941 *New York Times* Christmas editorial stated:
"The voice of Pius XII is a lonely voice in the silence and
darkness enveloping Europe." Its 1942 editorial referred to
him as "about the only ruler left on the continent of Europe
who dares to raise his voice at all.... The Pope put himself
squarely against Hitlerism."

Interestingly, the Gestapo's interpretation of the pope's
Christmas messages is clear: "In a manner never known
before ... the Pope has repudiated the National Socialist New
European Order [Nazism]. His speech is one long attack on
everything we stand for. Here he is clearly speaking on behalf
of the Jews."

It is historically inaccurate to charge Pope Pius XII with
"silence." His "silence" was a strategic approach to protect Jews and other refugees from Nazi terrorism. Whenever
protests were made, treatment of prisoners worsened immediately. To the very end, the pope was convinced that, should
he denounce Hitler publicly, there would be retaliation.

Pius XII was a diplomat engaged in the greatest Christian
rescue program in the history of the church. Editorials of the
time attest that Pius XII served as a beacon of hope for both

Jews and Christians. His many acts of mercy speak for themselves. He does not deserve to have his memory defamed by people who are opposed to the Catholic Church.

It is time to right the injustice toward a man who saved more Jews than any other person, including Oskar Schindler and Raoul Wallenberg. This was accomplished through Vatican directives suspending "cloister" regulations and allowing religious men and women to open their doors to protect Jews.

Several years ago, I interviewed Sister Maria Pucci — an eyewitness in the convent on Via Caboto, not far from the Jewish ghetto — who said: "We were young, frightened. We knew that if caught harboring Jews we would be shot by the Nazis or Fascists. Yet when twenty-five Jewish men, women, and children arrived, we opened our doors. What a scene that first day — they were desperate! We gave them what they needed, especially blankets to keep warm. Children were crying, hugging their mothers. Everyone was frightened. During air raids we all fled to the shelters. We prayed with the Jews. Our prayers were mixed with tears." When asked why the Sisters protected Jews, she answered: "Why? But these were our neighbors. We respected and loved them. We responded to the pope's plea to open our doors!"

Sister Lelia Orlandi recalled vividly the bitter night during a terrible November storm. Clara Coen-Capon and her husband, Luciano, with their one-year-old infant, knocked on the convent door in Cave, near Rome. The Sisters welcomed them. They were fully aware of the risk they were taking.

Pius XII deserves the title, "Righteous Gentile." His courageous acts during World War II are incontestable. In the February 26, 2001, issue of the *Weekly Standard*, Rabbi David G. Dalin writes about the vilification of the pontiff and defends him against his detractors.

No one can dismiss the praise Pius XII received from Jewish leaders and scholars as well as expressions of gratitude from Jewish chaplains and Holocaust survivors who bore personal witness to the assistance of the pope. Rabbi Dalin rightly states: "To deny the legitimacy of their gratitude to Pius XII is tantamount to denying the credibility of their personal testimony and judgment about the Holocaust itself. . . . To make Pius XII a target of our moral outrage against the Nazis, and to count Catholicism among the institutions delegitimized by the horror of the Holocaust, reveals a failure of historical understanding. Almost none of the recent books about Pius XII and the Holocaust are actually about Pius XII and the Holocaust. Their real topic proves to be an intra-Catholic argument about the direction of the Church today, with the Holocaust simply the biggest club available for liberal Catholics to use against traditionalists."

I also interviewed Cardinal Pietro Palazzini, who explained how Pius XII directed him to assist Jews. His testimony is clearly expressed: "Amidst the clash of arms, a voice could be heard — the voice of Pius XII. The assistance given to so many people could not have been possible without his moral support, which was much more than quiet consent" (*Il clero e l'occupazione di Roma*, 1995, 16).

Nor can we ignore the testimony by eyewitness Monsignor John Patrick Carroll-Abbing. His book *But for the Grace of God* provides information on his personal relationship with Pope Pius XII and the direct involvement of the pontiff with saving Rome's Jews.

Pius XII's charity had no bounds in the midst of hatred and destruction. He was personally interested in everyone who appealed to him for help to locate missing relatives. Requests for information came from every country in the world. This was the only archive in the world completely dedicated to transmitting news to the families of prisoners of war.

Mother Teresa Saccucci, superior general of the Religious Teachers Filippini, interviewed by the author of *La Chiesa e la Guerra* (1944), explained that the Sisters helped the Holy Father in the Information Office of the Vatican Secretariat of State. Mother Teresa recalled: "For this work in the Information Office, I had designated five or six Sisters with typewriters. . . . I did all I could to satisfy the pope's wishes."

In his book *Three Popes and the Jews* (1967), Jewish historian Pinchas Lapide states that the Vatican Information Office helped tens of thousands of Jews locate missing relatives in Europe. The *Canadian Jewish Chronicle* (January 26, 1940) published a story about Jacob Freedman, a Boston tailor who wrote to the State Department and the Red Cross for information about the fate of his sister and nephews in German-occupied Poland. They could not provide any information, so Freedman sought Pius XII's assistance. A few months later, he was assured that the members of his family were alive and well in Warsaw.

Pius XII publicly defended the Jews whenever the bishops informed him about Nazi atrocities. He did not want to jeopardize lives. He measured his statements carefully. He was a man of peace. Herbert L. Matthews, an American journalist in Rome, called Pope Pius XII "a peacemaker and conciliator" in the *New York Times* (October 15, 1945). Yet more than sixty years later, this pope is burdened by distortions and incoherent statements about his so-called "silence" during the Holocaust.

Michael Bobrow, an American Jewish journalist, whose cousin was saved by nuns in a convent in Belgium, wrote to me recently: "The canonization of Pope Pius XII would be an act of supreme justice, charity, and truth." Jewish physicist Albert Einstein wrote: "Only the Church stood squarely across the path of Hitler's campaign for suppressing the truth. I never had any special interest in the Church before, but now I feel a great affection and admiration because the Church alone has had the courage and persistence to stand for intellectual truth and moral freedom" (*Time* magazine, December 23, 1940).

It is important that the lessons of the Holocaust, although horrible to recall, be retold truthfully and accurately. It is equally important to recognize those who did all in their power to help the victims of Nazism. In fact, throughout Europe Pope Pius XII operated a vast underground railroad. While Italy was being devastated by Allied bombs, the Nazis were killing innocent people. Eighty-five percent of Italian Jews were saved. In occupied Europe, the Nazis killed 67 percent of the Jews. Millions of Christians did not escape Nazi terror during Hitler's attempt to exterminate all Jews. Nazism was pagan and racist.

It is imperative that Catholics and Jews respond to the allegations and indictments regarding Pope Pius XII. We must stop the calumnies about the silence of Pius XII and the misrepresentations that Christianity led directly to the Nazi death camps. Pius XII could not have taken a public stand against the Nazis without endangering the lives of other human beings. The thousands of Jews hidden in convents and monasteries would have been sent to concentration camps along with those who were trying to save them. How can Catholics ignore the truth?

Pius XII's voice was heard around the world. It was the voice of a tireless world leader whose contribution to humanity during the Holocaust is incontrovertible. He dedicated his efforts toward genuine reconciliation and regard for the sanctity of life. It is my fervent prayer that there be peace and love between Jews and Christians, and among all members of the human family.

Two

Defending the Pope

This I declare, that He alone is my refuge.
—Psalm 91

The Struggle for Peace

For almost twenty years the pope's voice served the Catholic Church with remarkable consistency, as he coordinated the church's efforts and cared for suffering humanity. Pope Pius XII desired peace, a peace that would "stand out in the centuries as a resolute advance in the affirmation of human dignity and of ordered liberty." His voice echoed over mountains and seas to the entire world. It vibrated peacefully, yet strongly, in the midst of the horrors of war.

While the Germans considered Pope Pius XII an implacable foe, he was hailed as the only voice, "a lonely voice" speaking out in Europe against the Nazi terror. He provided shelter to the persecuted Jews and other refugees. Hundreds of thousands were hidden in churches, convents, monasteries, schools. He protected Jews in attics, cellars, and barns, providing food and clothing, false papers, and money for escape. Pius XII served the Catholic Church with remarkable consistency, coordinating the church's efforts and caring for suffering humanity. By using diplomatic pressure, he accomplished more than the other world leaders combined.

Thanks to the Jesuit historians Robert Graham, Pierre Blet, Angelo Martini, and Burkhart Schneider, World War II documents regarding the extraordinary peace efforts and the humanitarian work of the Holy See may be found in the *Actes et documents du Saint Siège relatifs à la Seconde Guerre Mondiale* published in twelve volumes by Libreria Editrice Vaticana from 1965 to 1981. As Jews and Catholics strive for brotherhood, these five thousand documents will serve to enlighten the world about Pope Pius XII's activities, help readers understand the injustice toward the memory of Pius XII, and spread the truth about the Catholic Church.

With the opening of the Vatican Archives, new evidence contradicts the prejudice and insensitivity of some writers with regard to the record of the Catholic Church during the Holocaust. How can we ignore the testimony of contemporary witnesses? Justice demands a re-evaluation of the attacks against Pius XII claiming "silence," "moral culpability," or "anti-Semitism." Israeli attorney general Gideon Hausner testified: "The Pope himself intervened personally in support of the Jews of Rome."

Why do Catholics ignore the unscrupulous manipulations of the truth? Do Catholics lack courage to fight for justice? Should Catholics continue to tolerate a sustained campaign of denigration of Pope Pius XII?

One story of compassion and love is an inspiration. It began in 1939, when 150 German Jews fled from Germany armed with visas for the United States. In order to obtain transportation, they sought refuge in Italy. But not long after their arrival, the war had expanded. Jews were immediately arrested and placed in chains. Entrusted to Father Francesco Sacco, for three years these prisoners were interned in the town of Campagna, near the Bay of Salerno, living in a monastery and gratefully enjoying the loving care of the local residents. Recent documentation shows that Pius XII personally sent financial assistance.

When the Allies bombed the monastery, the Jews fled to the mountains. Soon the Nazis took control of the town and began shooting Italians. Although hidden in the mountains, the Jews learned that the Italians were without medical assistance. Among them were four Jewish surgeons, who returned to the town to care for the many casualties. These Jews knew the Nazis were searching for them; if caught, they would have been shot or deported. Yet they did not hesitate. Without medical equipment, they performed forty major operations in two days and saved Italian lives. Documents reveal that financial assistance was supplied by the Vatican.[1]

There were numerous Jewish petitions for Vatican help. Countless letters arrived each day requesting the Holy Father's help in locating missing persons and prisoners of war. Among the many requests for assistance, Pius XII received a telegram from Rabbi Isaac Herzog, chief rabbi of Jerusalem, who petitioned for the Vatican's help in locating a Swedish rabbi arrested in 1942. The *New York Times* published the pope's reply promising "to do all in his personal power to aid persecuted Jews in Europe." Another telegram from Grand Rabbi Israel Herzog in Egypt arrived. He requested help on behalf of Jews interned in the Ferramonti concentration camp in Italy: "Egyptian Jews express profound gratitude Holy See for generous charitable activity continually exercised in pro-

---

1. This story comes from an article published in *Life* magazine (November 1, 1943). What the article does not state is that Bishop Palatucci wrote to Pius XII requesting help to care for these prisoners.

tection their European co-religionists and alleviation their sufferings. Have learned with anxiety measures contemplated for deporting refugee Jews at present interned Ferramonti and beg Holy See intervene in order these may remain in Italy under vigilant protection Holy See whom Jews of world consider their historic protector in oppression."[2]

In 1954, Pius XII became gravely ill and considered abdication of his office. Only when the doctors assured him that he would recover and would soon be able to resume his duties did he resign himself to remain as pope. In fact, he continued his mission and gave four more years of fruitful service to the church.

During his final illness, when he could no longer celebrate Holy Mass, Pius XII repeated constantly the *Anima Christi*. According to Padre Agostino (*Diario*, 225), after Pope Pius XII died, the saintly Padre Pio — one of the most charismatic figures of the twentieth century — was consoled "by a vision of the former pontiff in his heavenly home."

The Option for the Poor

Sister Pascalina Lehnert, Eugenio Pacelli's loyal and faithful housekeeper from 1923 to 1958 — the period when he was nuncio in Germany until his death — respected his wishes throughout her thirty-five years of service. As part of her service, she implemented his wishes with regard to helping the poor of Rome.

---

2. Additional information concerning the Italian concentration camps of Campagna and Ferramonti-Tarsia was revealed in the 1999 book entitled *Bad Times, Good People: A Holocaust Survivor Recounts His Life in Italy during WWII* (1999). The author is Walter Wolff, a German Jew who lived through the Holocaust.

In her 1982 memoirs, *Ich durfte ihm dienen: Erinnerungen an Papst Pius XII* (I was permitted to serve Pope Pius XII), Sister Pascalina tells her own story.[3] In the January 2008 issue of *Inside the Vatican*, historian John Jay Hughes writes: "Sister Pascalina emerges from these pages as a woman of exceptional energy and great organizational talent. During World War II she ran an enormous charitable work, which sent letters and food to prisoners of war. After the war she continued this work for devastated Germany sending (to Cardinal Faulhaber of Munich especially) not only provisions, but bicycles, motorcycles, and cars. She was even able to organize the erection of temporary barrack churches in her homeland."

Sister Pascalina's statement that the pope explicitly warned the Germans against Adolf Hitler in 1929, four years before the dictator came into power on January 30, 1933, is authentic: "When asked if Hitler could perhaps help the German people, Pacelli shook his head and said: 'Who among you has at least read his horrifying book, *Mein Kampf?* I would be very much mistaken in thinking that all this could end well.' The future Pope Pius XII could not understand why even highly competent Germans did not share his totally negative judgment."

Sister Pascalina was in contact with the Jews who insisted that Pius XII avoid any public action for fear of aggravating the situation in Rome, which was occupied by the Nazis in 1943. In her deposition (Session 163, March 17, 1972) Sister Pascalina wrote: "The Pope not only opened the doors of the Vatican to protect the persecuted, but he encouraged convents and monasteries to offer hospitality. The Vatican provided

---

3. Her well-documented story has now been published by Martha Schad in *Gottes mächtige Dienerin: Schwester Pascalina und Papst Pius XII* (God's powerful servant: Sister Pascalina and Pius XII) (2007).

provisions for these people. The accusation that Pius XII was indifferent to the needs of the victims is without foundation. He ordered me to spend his inheritance and personal funds to provide for those who wished to leave Italy and go to Canada, Brazil, or elsewhere. Note that $800 was needed for each person who emigrated. Many times the Pope would ask me to deliver to Jewish families a sealed envelope containing $1,000 or more."

Reuben Resnick, American director of the Committee to Help Jews in Italy, declared: "All the members of the Catholic hierarchy in Italy, from cardinals to priests, saved the lives of thousands of Jews, men, women, and children who were hosted and hidden in convents, churches, and other religious institutions." Sister Pascalina Lehnert confirmed Pope Pius XII's direct role in this protective work.

The Voice of Truth and Justice

Pius XII pleaded publicly for peace on August 24, 1939: "Nothing is lost through peace; all can be lost through war." He desired peace, a peace "that may stand out in the centuries as a resolute advance in the affirmation of human dignity and of ordered liberty."

Pius XII was a saintly man, a man of peace and compassion. He strongly condemned the anti-Semitic persecutions, the oppression of invaded lands, and the inhuman conduct of the Nazis. He urged the Christian restoration of family life and education, the reconstruction of society, the equality of nations, the suppression of hate propaganda, and the formation of an international organization for disarmament and maintenance of peace. He was a champion of peace, freedom, human dignity. He encouraged Catholics to look on Christians and Jews as their brothers and sisters, all children of a common Father.

Speaking to a group of Jewish leaders during his visit to the United States, Pope John Paul II stated that documents "reveal ever more clearly and convincingly how deeply Pius XII felt the tragedy of the Jewish people, and how hard and effectively he worked to assist them." His Holiness called for "genuine brotherhood" between Christians and Jews.

During the early twentieth century, the world was plagued with racism, nationalism, and militarism long before Eugenio Pacelli became pope. Pius XII was a unique figure in modern history. Throughout his priestly life, he was admired by Catholics and non-Catholics. Studies of his papal documents rekindle confidence in God and in the future. He restored church prestige and provided the faithful and the world with extraordinary leadership.

This pope had to deal with Adolf Hitler and the Holocaust, Benito Mussolini and Fascism, the occupation of Rome by the Nazis, the development of atomic warfare, and the spread of Communism across Eastern Europe. He enunciated moral principles, avoided provocations, strove for impartiality among belligerents, and issued information about Nazi atrocities through Vatican Radio and *L'Osservatore Romano*.

Vatican Radio has been the daily "voice" of the pontiffs — a bridge uniting the Shepherd with his flock. Even today it announces the Christian message freely and efficiently and links the center of Catholicism with the countries of the world. Any judgment of Pius XII must look closely at these broadcasts. Vatican Radio has enjoyed a long history of world recognition and credibility, supporting both the sacred and secular objectives of the church during religious and political turmoil. The opening of the Vatican Archives has already proven that accusations against Pius XI and Pius XII are baseless. Documents reveal that as Secretary of State Pacelli was not sympathetic toward Hitler.

Shortly after the pope's death, Secretary of State Cardinal Domenico Tardini wrote: "Pius XII will go down in history as a Pontiff who was a wise reformer and brave innovator. He was a voice of truth and of justice. Pius XII was a holy person, a symbol of mercy and of hope during a period of lies, despair, and hatred. Everyone appreciated his intelligence, his extraordinary capacity to comprehend the dangers of Nazism, and his efforts to alleviate the sufferings of humanity. His messages attempted to unite the world. His contemporaries listened to his inspiring words, as he spoke of brotherhood, of love, and of peace at a time of spiritual poverty and material destruction of exceptional dimensions" (Domenico Tardini, *Pio XII*, 1958).

Pius XII was engaged in the greatest Christian rescue program in the history of the church. Editorials of the time attest to the fact that he saved hundreds of thousands of Jews and Christians from death in the concentration camps and served as a beacon of hope throughout his pontificate.

Speaking to about five hundred delegates from forty-two countries who were in Rome for the eighth congress of the World Medical Association (1958), Pius XII stated: "There can be no doubt, especially in view of the horrors and immense suffering caused by modern war, that to unleash it without just cause ... would constitute a crime worthy of the most severe national and international sanctions." In his reference to "a just cause," the pope spoke of a war "forced upon one by an evident and extremely grave injustice that

in no way can be avoided." He said that "the question of
the legitimacy of atomic, bacteriological, and chemical war"
could not be posed as a matter of principle, "except when
it must be judged indispensable to defend oneself in the circumstances indicated." He had a sincere predilection for the
medical profession: "Like the priest and the Church, a doctor must be a friend and must help humanity; he must be a
true collaborator of God in the defense and development of
creation."

In his last discourse to surgeons, five days before his death,
he continued to teach the value and the beauty of one's soul:
"How many souls found serenity in your capable hands! How
many were helped by your science and art! Always recognize
that your mission can and must go beyond the body and teach
those entrusted to you to appreciate interior beauty."

The following excerpt, written by hand, was also part of a
discourse to an international group of doctors: "How exalted,
how worthy of all honour is the character of your profession!
The doctor has been appointed by God Himself (cf. Eccli.
38:1) to minister to the needs of suffering humanity. He who
created that fever-consumed or mangled frame, now in your
hands, who loves it with an eternal love, confided to you the
ennobling charge of restoring it to health. You will bring to
the sickroom and the operating table something of the charity of God, of the love and tenderness of Christ, the Master
Physician of soul and body."

Pius XII was the first pope to leave such an abundance of
writings and discourses. Throughout his life Pacelli continued
scholarly pursuits. In 1943, for example, in a discourse to the
Pontifical Academy of Science, he forecast the development of
atomic energy and discussed the disintegration that uranium
undergoes when bombarded by neutrons. The pope expressed

the hope that its force would be harnessed for the service of man and not released for his destruction. On September 19, 1945, the *New York Times* wrote: "Pope Pius XII this morning received Sir Alexander Fleming and discussed with him new uses of penicillin. The discoverer of penicillin presented the Pontiff a plate for cultivating mold to be used in research. Sir Alexander, after a twenty-minute audience, declared he was astonished at the Pope's knowledge of his discovery."

In 1951 Pius XII spoke on modern science and the proofs for the existence of God. On another occasion, he addressed the International Astronomical Union and spoke on the histopathology of the central nervous system. His speeches ranged from international penal law, toleration, psychiatry, and clinical psychology, to medical genetics, ophthalmology, urology, medico-moral problems, as well as accountancy and economics, moral guidance, and statistics. Most of his speeches were in French or Italian, but a few were in Spanish, German, English, or Latin.

"A Miracle Took Place"

Pius XII's virtuous life speaks for itself. On December 13, 1954, a picture story entitled "Years of a Great Pope" appeared in *Life* magazine. The author states that Pius XII was deserving of the title "Great Pope" because he sought "peace for the world and the spirit" during World War II. For almost two decades, he was "unbending, working with devotion and all the skills of diplomacy to mitigate the burdens of a beleaguered world. He defended and fortified the Church, condemned Nazi racialism as antireligious, stemmed the Communist tide by firm intervention in the 1948 Italian elections, created new cardinals from all over the globe, and proclaimed the dogma of the Assumption of the Virgin Mary."

In 1954, the world looked with pride and admiration at the many-sided career of Pope Pius XII, who, in his own agonized generation, was already recognized as a "Great Pope." Many appealed to him for help to locate missing relatives. Requests for information came from all over the world. This was the only archive in the world completely dedicated to transmitting news to the families of prisoners of war.

Fifty years later, I interviewed Carlo Sestieri, a Jewish survivor, who was hidden in the Vatican. In a letter to me he suggested that "only the Jews who were persecuted understand why the Holy Father could not publicly denounce the Nazi-Fascist government. Without doubt — he stated — it helped avoid worse disasters."

Who can say that Pius XII's voice was not heard prior to and during the period of the Holocaust? It was heard through Vatican Radio. The *London Times* (October 1, 1942) praised Pius XII: "There is no room for doubt. He condemns the worship of force ... and the persecution of the Jewish race." The *Tablet* reported that Nazi leader Goebbels issued pamphlets in many languages condemning Pius XII as a "pro-Jewish Pope" (October 24, 1942).

Pius XII's charity and love prevailed. He was concerned that a public condemnation would result in retaliation and the loss of more lives. His "silence" accompanied a powerful action in defense of the Jews. Herbert L. Matthews, an American journalist in Rome, called Pope Pius XII "a peacemaker and conciliator" (*New York Times*, October 15, 1945). Jewish scholar Jenö Levai, testifying at the Adolf Eichmann Nazi War Crime Trials, stated that "the one person [Pope Pius XII] who did more than anyone else to halt the dreadful crime and alleviate its consequences, is today made the scapegoat for the failures of others" (*Hungarian Jewry and the Papacy,* 1968). "A miracle took place here!" is a famous phrase of Y. Bankover "Hamèsh Shanìm." It was printed in *Diario di un soldato ebreo:* "In the midst of the general destruction that characterized the war zones, Rome remained intact. 'A miracle took place here!': thousands of Jews were safe and sound. The Church, the religious houses, monks, sisters, and above all the Pontiff, have worked in an extraordinary way to save Jews from the clutches of the Nazis and their collaborators, the Italian Fascists. While endangering their own lives, they succeeded with great efforts in hiding and feeding the Jews during the German occupation of Rome. Some religious paid the price with their lives to accomplish this (e.g., Don Pietro Pappagallo and Don Giuseppe Morosini). The entire Church participated with devotion in this effort. Not less important and decisive in saving lives was the help given by the population of Rome. The citizens generally hid Jews in their homes, feeding them with the little food they had. Every Jewish family that returned home after the Germans left found their own house in order, thanks to the Christian citizens who, notwithstanding the dangers encountered, guarded the homes of the Jews under the very eyes of the Gestapo."

In September 1943, a representative from the World Jewish Congress reported to the pope that approximately four thousand Jews and Yugoslav nationals who had been in internment camps were removed to an area that was under the control of Yugoslav partisans. As such, they were out of immediate danger. The report went on to say: "I feel sure that the efforts of your Grace and the Holy See have brought about this fortunate result, and I should like to express to the

Holy See and yourself the warmest thanks of the World Jewish Congress. The Jews concerned will probably not yet know by what agency their removal from danger has been secured, but when they do they will be indeed grateful."

Two months later, Isaac Herzog (chief rabbi of Palestine) wrote to Pope Pius XII expressing his "sincere gratitude and deep appreciation for so kind an attitude toward Israel and for such valuable assistance given by the Catholic Church to the endangered Jewish people." Jewish communities in Chile, Uruguay, and Bolivia also sent similar offers of thanks to the pope.

A precursor of Vatican II, Pope Pius XII refused to identify Christianity with Western culture or with a particular political system. He successfully saved the lives of thousands of Jews, a feat unmatched by any other world leader during World War II. In the words of Cardinal Tarcisio Bertone: "He was a man who, by his personal holiness, shines as a luminous witness of the Catholic priesthood and of the papacy."

Three

The Cause for Canonization

Do you want peace? Change the heart, and the world will be changed. Root out greed and plant charity.... Once you have avoided evil and done good, then seek peace and follow it.

— Pius XII's final message of peace

Since the beginning of the year 2005, there has been an increased interest in the beatification of Pope Pius XII among Catholics throughout the world. Pius XII was a man of deep faith and extraordinary charity. No other head of state or religious leader before, during, or after World War II did as much as Eugenio Pacelli to save Jews fleeing from Nazi persecution.

There are volumes of depositions for the beatification of Pius XII. His sanctity has been recorded. He was a humble person who did not want his many good works and accomplishments revealed. Respecting his wishes, Sister Pascalina Lehnert, his housekeeper, implemented the pope's charitable works and served him faithfully from 1923 to 1958. In her deposition, Sister Pascalina clearly stated that Pius XII did not issue a formal condemnation of Nazism because the German and Austrian bishops dissuaded him from making additional protests that would undoubtedly have aggravated Hitler. They feared increased retaliation.

And there was retaliation. During the persecution against Catholics, the Nazis not only destroyed churches and closed schools, but also arrested priests and Catholic leaders, who were sent to concentration camps. All the protests of the Holy See were reported in a volume published in Germany in 1965 (*Der Notenwechsel zwischen dem Heiligen Stuhl und der Deutschen Reichsregierung,* edited by Dieter Albrecht [Mainz: Matthias-Grunewald-Verlag, 1965].

Pius XII's pontificate left a lasting mark on the history of the Catholic Church. His life was one of action, inspired by profound piety. He brought consolation, peace, and encouragement everywhere. He instituted numerous liturgical reforms: the evening Mass, the new Eucharistic fast regulations, and increased lay participation in liturgical functions. The Eucharistic Liturgy was the source from which Pius XII drew strength and wisdom to lead the world.

Devotion to Mary

Pius XII has been called the "Pope of Mary" for his great devotion to the Mother of God, evidenced in the infallible definition of the Assumption. Furthermore, the consecration of Russia and of the whole world to the Immaculate Heart of Mary, the solemn proclamation of the Marian Year, the institution of the feast of the Queenship of Mary, and the proclamation of the centenary of the Apparitions of Our Blessed Lady to St. Bernadette were also made by Pius XII.

Pope Pius XII's devotion to Mary stemmed from early childhood. In the house there was a shrine to Our Lady where Eugenio would kneel with his mother. Sometimes, when his mother was busy, Eugenio would go to the shrine and pray by himself. One day she asked her son what he was doing there. He said: "Why, Mother, I talk to the Mother of Jesus."

Rights for Women

Pope Pius XII's voice was among the greatest male advocates of women's rightful position in today's world; he called woman "the crown of creation and, in a certain sense, its masterpiece." The pope gave his views on woman's role in modern life in a series of talks to various groups of women. He spoke on "The Role of Young Women," "Woman Today and Tomorrow," "Woman in Industry," and "Woman's Duties in Social and Political Life."

In his 1956 talk "The Crown of Creation" he stated: "The issues confronting women are not mere matters of politics or education or legal status, but pertain to women's nature, dignity, and destiny. Woman is equal with man, equal in dignity, equal in eternal destiny, equal in pursuit of sanctity. Man is not superior to woman or woman to man. They are complementary. By the manner of his birth, Jesus ennobled both sexes. He was a man born of woman."

Pius XII recognized the breadth of women's horizons. "Every woman is called to be a mother, a mother in the physical sense or a mother in a sense more spiritual and exalted, yet real nevertheless.... There is no field of human activity which must remain closed to women. Her horizons reach out to regions of science, politics, labor, the arts and sports ... and women should seek education to develop their highest human potential in all areas.... In questions of woman's dignity, her honor and integrity, the protection and education of the child, who better than a woman can understand what is needed?"

A Spiritual Life

Pacelli's prayerfulness was noted throughout his life. Very reserved, he did not speak about his personal spirituality, but all those who approached him realized that he was in constant union with God.

Those who worked closely with Pius XII claim that he lived a life of exemplary temperance and mortification. He was an ascetic, and practiced every virtue in an extraordinary way. He wanted only simple food. His meals were that of a poor person. He ate very little and did not eat desserts. He did not use alcoholic beverages or tobacco. Even though he needed special foods, during the war years he forbade any exceptions for his own meals. His weight was reduced to 125 pounds.

He did not want his apartment heated because the thousands of refugees hidden by the Vatican could not have their rooms heated. He slept only four hours each day, after working until two in the morning and getting up at 6:00 a.m. Even when the time for fasting before receiving Holy Communion was reduced, he continued to observe the original fast regulations.

Solidarity with the Oppressed

Regarding Pius XII's so-called "silence," most historians agree that he could not publicly denounce Hitler. Having the responsibility for the universal church, the pope did what his conscience told him and worked in practical ways for the spiritual and physical good of so many. Under his direction the Catholic Church saved the lives of Jews, Fascists, anti-Fascists, and Germans.

Claims are unfounded that Pius XII was not explicit enough in his 1942 Christmas address when he spoke about the "hundreds of thousands who, without any fault of their own, sometimes only by reason of their nationality or race, are marked down for death or gradual extinction." Anyone who understood the pontiff's precarious position in 1942 and the ever-present danger of reprisals as well as anyone who read and heard his addresses knew exactly what the pope was saying. In his encyclical *Summi Pontificatus* he condemned racism and totalitarianism and defended Jews specifically, expressing solidarity with them on October 20, 1939. The Allies considered it so important that they dropped thousands of copies of it on German territory. The Nazis reacted, understanding that it was directed against Germany.

Pius XII's statement was clear in its condemnation of the treatment of Poles and Jews. In their pastoral letter of February 21, 1943, the Dutch bishops cited Pius XII's message as their inspiration for speaking out: "We would fail in our duty if we did not publicly raise our voice against the injustice to which such a large part of our people is being subjected. In this we are following the path indicated by our Holy Father the Pope, who in his latest Christmas message declared: 'The Church would be untrue to herself... if she turned a deaf ear to her children's anguished cries which reach her from every class of the human family.... In the midst of all the injustice and anguish, our sympathy goes out in a very special manner ... to the Jews, and to our brethren in the Catholic faith who are of Jewish descent.' "

In July 1944, the American Jewish Committee and other Jewish organizations organized a rally in Manhattan, to protest the deportation of Hungarian Jews. The president of the Committee said: "We have seen how great was the work of the Holy Father in saving the Jews in Italy. We also learned from various sources that this great Pope has tried to help and save the lives of Jews in Hungary." Pius XII's example, as manifested in his concern for the Jews and for all victims of the Nazis, the prisoners of war, the homeless and displaced persons have added to his words the testimony of his actions in a world that knew no peace.

A Fighter for Peace

Eugenio Pacelli was the pope during a tragic period of history. He was a model of sanctity. The miracle of Pius XII is that of the house built upon the rock (Matt. 7:24), which he kept intact in silence and, by virtue of silence, it was capable of providing shelter and protection. When he died on October 9, 1958, an editorial, "Fighter for Peace," in the *Los Angeles Examiner,* expressed the sentiments of Catholics and non-Catholics: "Pius XII was known as 'the Pope of Peace.' He called himself a *fighter for peace*. His self-description was more accurate, for the years of his reign, beginning in March 1939, were those of the horrible violence of war or the stealth and treachery of Communist evil. It was in these and through these continuous ordeals that the gentle and ascetic scholar became God's warrior; a bulwark against despair, a magnificent *fighter for peace,* a repository of the hopes of mankind. Never, during these troubled years, did Pius XII lose his gift of gracious beneficence. Whether the audiences were large or small, he conveyed a sense of intimacy and understanding. His gifts to them were hope and courage. This *fighter for peace* is now in peace with God."

Some Testimonies

Among the many testimonies that Pope Pius XII did care for and save many Jews is that of Dr. Kessler. He was saved in the Vatican and he did not fail to acknowledge his debt of gratitude toward the Roman pontiff.

Dr. Kessler explained that during World War II, he was hidden in the Vatican and protected from the Nazis by the pope. He learned much about the Catholic religion because, while hidden there, he was given the run of the whole Vatican: grounds, buildings, museums, libraries.

Recently, Mordecai Paldiel, former director of the Yad Vashem Museum, selected the stories of some three hundred Christian clerics, both male and female, who acted with humanity and generosity toward Jews in their hour of peril. He writes that the motivation of rescuers of Jews was compassion for their sufferings coupled with a Christian duty to help others in need. He acknowledges that the thousands of Jews hidden in religious establishments throughout Italy were there with the knowledge and consent of Pope Pius XII and concludes that the "Righteous clergy" can serve as role models for a new and constructive relationship between Judaism and Christianity.

Other people dedicated to the cause of rescuing Jews during those terrible days have paid tribute to the efforts of Pius XII. For example, John W. Phele, executive director of the U.S. War Refugee Board, wrote just after the war ended in 1945: "The Catholic clergy saved and protected many thousands and the Vatican rendered invaluable assistance to the Board and to the persecuted in Nazi hands."

Sir Francis Osborne, a non-Catholic British diplomat in the Vatican from 1936 to 1947, had this to say (*Times* of London,

May 20, 1963): "Pius XII was the most warm, humane,
kindly, generous, sympathetic (and, incidentally, saintly) character that it has been my privilege to meet.... Without the
slightest doubt, he would have been ready and glad to give
his life to redeem humanity from its consequences — and this
quite irrespective of nationality or Faith."

After fifty years, the faithful continue to affirm this testimony. I quote several messages from among the thousands I
have received:

"We were all there, in Germany, during World War II. I
am so pleased, and so are my friends, that finally the truth is
printed; the truth we always knew. It was in 1958, in Toronto,
that I happened to have a conversation with a Jew. As I told
him I was Catholic, he immediately said, 'Oh, you have such
a wonderful Pope [Pius XII]. He has done so much for us
Jews!' Where are these voices today?" (Liselotte Eschenauer,
Toronto, Canada).

"I was in Rome during World War II and I am personally
aware of the extraordinary efforts of the Church under Pope
Pius XII to assist Jews and save Jewish children from their
enemies. All of the recent efforts to defame His Holiness and
to change history are political and can be fought best by ele-
vating him to sainthood as early as is possible" (Francis Paul
DiBlasi, Jr., Naples, Florida).

"While I was growing up in Germany before and during
World War II, Pope Pius XII was a source of constant strength
to Catholics living during those times. Because of his example
and support, bishops and priests spoke out and resisted the
regime. My parish in Berlin lost at least one or two young
priests to concentration camps. The present campaign against
this holy pope is really just an attack on the Catholic Church
brought by people who were not even alive and did not live in

Germany during these terrible times and who have no clue as to the conditions under which everyone lived and suffered" (Sigrid Ruedel Crane, Vienna, Virginia).

"As a Roman Catholic whose great grandfather was Jewish, I have a special reason to support the beatification of Pope Pius XII. I grew up with a lot of resentment and mixed feelings hearing about the so-called Hitler's Pope. Now that I am older and have seen the light, I have seen the vicious lies that have been spread. I would ask the future St. Pius XII to forgive us for not defending him. Thank you. Pius XII, pray for us!" (Timothy Joseph Andries, Breaux Bridge, Louisiana).

Pope Pius XII weighed everything in light of gospel revelations and Christian traditions. He restored church prestige and provided the faithful and the world with extraordinary leadership.

Challenges and Injustices

Pius XII's long pontificate has been seriously challenged by classic anti-Catholicism, which has expressed itself in attacks on his papacy. This is a serious misreading of a great pontiff. Philip Jenkins, a member of the Episcopal Church, in his scholarly book *The New Anti-Catholicism: The Last Acceptable Prejudice,* contends that today's anti-Catholicism stems from the radical social changes in the 1960s. These led to the rise of interest groups such as feminists and homosexual activists who oppose the church. He believes that the mainstream media downplay even the most violent anti-Catholic actions and affirms: "Catholics and Catholicism are at the receiving end of a great deal of startling vituperation in contemporary America."

The campaign of vilification against Pius XII that began in the 1960s continues today. His detractors claim that he lacked courage, human compassion, and a sense of moral rectitude. Hostile attacks by the media replace the historical record that showed him as a great leader. In contrast to the esteem Pius XII enjoyed until his death, his reputation today suffers many unjust attacks. However, according to Michael Novak, these critics "are deflecting attention from themselves.... Today's charges against Pope Pius XII cannot stand scrutiny." What Pius XII did for the Jews directly and indirectly through his diplomatic representatives and the bishops is well documented.

Pope Pius XII is a unique figure in modern history, an extraordinary man who fulfilled his duties with courage and great wisdom, and who was in his personal life an exemplary Christian, priest, bishop, cardinal, and pope. Indeed, the voice of the people is the voice of God. *Vox populi, Vox Dei!* The Romans gave Pope Pius XII the title *Defensor Civitatis;* his contemporaries throughout the world acclaimed him *Pastor Angelicus.*

Although he is one of the most distinguished prelates ever to serve the church, Pius XII has been subjected to more unjust criticism than any of his predecessors. He continues to be vilified and praised, judged and defended. His papacy achieved a wider respect than any since the Reformation. He restored church prestige and provided the faithful and the world with extraordinary leadership. Pope Pius XII's aspirations toward truth and goodness and his extraordinary achievements may be considered one of the great events of the twentieth century. Many of his contemporaries considered him a saint. Long after his detractors are forgotten, Eugenio Pacelli will go down in history as one of the great religious leaders of his age, or indeed any age.

The Attitude of the Jews

As the Vatican moves toward the beatification of Pope Pius XII, some prominent American Jewish leaders continue to insist that the church desist from such action, asserting that Pius was guilty of not doing enough to prevent Hitler's genocide of Jews during the Holocaust.

In reality, the wartime pope did far more to save Jews than did any other leaders of the day, including people like Franklin Delano Roosevelt and Winston Churchill, who, unlike Pius, had enormous military assets at their command. Yet for some incomprehensible reason, it is Pius, the only world leader who made sustained efforts to save Jews during the Holocaust, who is the scapegoat for the world's failure to act forthrightly in the face of evil.

In an effort to counteract the inaccuracies of some historians, I have gathered documentation that proves how outrageously incorrect are the misrepresentations about Pope Pius XII's "silence" and "anti-Semitism." Consider the testimonials of Jewish leaders of his day thanking him for his efforts and the gratitude that five thousand Jews saved during the Nazi occupation of Rome evince for the pope. They understood that the pope had to be prudent while moving behind the scenes to protect as many Jews as he possibly could. Had he taken a more public and provocative stand, he would have infuriated Hitler and invited Nazi retaliation against the Vatican, thereby endangering the lives of thousands of Jews who, at the pope's direction, were hidden in 155 convents and monasteries in Rome alone.

Consider Pius's own words during those terrible days. On January 5, 1943, in response to Roosevelt's letter of December 31, 1942 — the most crucial moment in the war — the pope expressed his readiness to collaborate with him to achieve peace. "While maintaining this prayerful watch... it is Our undeviating program to do everything in Our power to alleviate the countless sufferings arising from this tragic conflict." Furthermore, President Roosevelt wrote on August 3, 1944, to Myron C. Taylor, his personal representative at the Vatican: "I should like you to take the occasion to express to His Holiness my deeply felt appreciation of the frequent action which the Holy See has taken on its own initiative in its generous and merciful efforts to render assistance to the victims of racial and religious persecutions."

Or consider that on June 25, 1944, Pius XII telegraphed the following protest message to Admiral Miklós von Nagybánya Horthy, the pro-Nazi ruler of Hungary, in which he spoke of the sufferings endured by hundreds of thousands "on account of their national or racial origin.... We appeal to your noble feelings, in the full trust that Your Serene Highness will do everything in Your power to save many unfortunate people from further pain and sorrow."

Then there is this more personal account of Pius XII's interaction with a young Jewish man: "During an audience along with numerous other people, a young Jew told Pius XII about a group of shipwrecked Jewish refugees, saved by Italian warships in the Aegean Sea, who were then starving in a prisoner of war camp on an island. The Pope listened carefully and showed concern about the conditions of the Jewish prisoners. Pius XII then said to him, 'You have done well to come and tell me this. Come back tomorrow with a written report and

give it to the secretary of state who is dealing with this question.... My son, I hope you will always be proud to be a Jew!'
... Pius XII lifted his hands to bless him, then stopped, smiled, touched the young man's head with his fingers, and lifted him from his kneeling position. The Pope raised his voice, so that everyone in the hall could hear it clearly: 'My son, whether you are worthier than others only the Lord knows, but believe me, you are at least as worthy as every other human being that lives on our earth! And now, my Jewish friend, go with the protection of the Lord, and never forget, you must always be proud to be a Jew!' "

In response to the inaccurate and unjust statement by Shmuley Boteach on April 15, and that of April 17, 2007, by Etgar Lefkovits, both in the online edition of the *Jerusalem Post,* I submit the following testimony published on April 28, 1944, in the *Palestine Post* (the present *Jerusalem Post*) and headlined "A Papal Audience in Wartime." It was signed by a "refugee"; a footnote states that the article's author arrived in Palestine on the ship *Nyassa.* This article, published by a young German Jew, notes Pope Pius XII's deep concern for the "Chosen People." It is significant because it shows the attention and great love with which the pontiff regarded the Jews.

Documents show that renowned Jewish contemporaries of Pius XII strongly defended him — among them, Israeli foreign minister Golda Meir: "When fearful martyrdom came to our people in the decade of Nazi terror, the voice of the Pope was raised for the victims." Nor can Albert Einstein's statement (*Time* magazine, December 23, 1940) be ignored: "Only the Church stood squarely across the path of Hitler's campaign for suppressing the truth."

Jewish historian Pinchas Lapide tells how Pope Pius XII sent his papal nuncio in Berlin to visit Hitler in Berchtesgaden to plead for the Jews. That interview ended when Hitler smashed a glass at the nuncio's feet. From Hitler's reaction, the pope was convinced that public pronouncements would have sealed the fate of many more Jews. Indeed, after this incident, Hitler, who often raged to his henchmen against the pope for protecting Jews, conceived a plot — fortunately never realized — to kidnap Pius XII from the Vatican and bring him to Germany.

Whatever the reason, I implore modern-day Jews of good will and open minds to take another hard look at the evidence concerning the wartime pope. If they do, I am convinced that they will come to the conclusion that Pius XII is blameless of the charges against him. Indeed, Pius deserves to be acclaimed as a "Righteous Gentile" for his courageous efforts that saved thousands of Jews from certain death.

A Saint in Our Midst

Cardinal Angelo Roncalli (the future Pope John XXIII) venerated Pius XII. In fact, on October 11, 1958, in his eulogy in St. Mark's Basilica, Venice, he recalled the magisterium of Pius XII, who "adapted himself to modern thought and progress. History would recall his example, his messages. As leader of the Catholic Church, he would be listed among the great and most popular of modern history." He concluded with a prayer: "You were the *Pastor Angelicus* and you guided us along the path of eternal life; you were the defender of our country, in our most tragic hours; ... bless our homes, families, priests, our poor, our suffering, our children. Oh, unforgettable, saintly Father, *sit super nos semper benedictio tua. Amen.*"

There is no doubt that the distinctive spiritual dimension of Pius XII's pontificate has been underestimated, especially by the media. Perhaps the words of His Eminence Cardinal Fiorenzo Angelini, who recalls his July 1943 encounter with the pope in the midst of the ruins of Allied bombings, will enlighten the public: "What unifies the Magisterium of Pope Pius XII and explains his firmness in confronting error, is his spontaneous charity toward the weak, the persecuted, and the needy; as well as his attention to all problems of modern society.... He was not only a great *man;* he was a great *man of God.*"

On the occasion of the first anniversary of Pius XII's death in October 1959, Cardinal Angelini received a mandate from the Catholic Doctors Association in Italy to contact Pope John XXIII. "After Pius XII's death," Angelini wrote, "the admiration and the devotion for this unforgettable Pontiff changed to profound veneration as testified by the National Assembly in Catania. Many of us have interceded for spiritual and temporal blessings. Your Holiness, I trust that the humble prayer expressed by thousands of doctors on the first anniversary of his death will result in his glorification and beatification."

Among the many reports on physical and spiritual graces received through the intercession of Pius XII, Nicholas D. Wehri from Ohio commented: "I support the beatification of Pius XII. I prayed to him once and told him about my learning disability. An instant spiritual healing filled my soul. It was incredible. That was all the proof I needed." Miracles have been attributed to his intercession in various parts of the world. Edvige Carboni lived in Rome during the entire pontificate of Pius XII. In her correspondence she repeatedly stated: "Our Pope is truly a saint! During the war we suffered so much! If it had not been for the help of the Holy Father, we would have all died of hunger ... but the Pope came to us and to all Rome with help, giving us bread, and also clothing. Our Pope is a saint! Love him."

Conclusion

Documents confirm that Pius XII was indeed a champion of peace, freedom, and human dignity, a pastor who encouraged Catholics to look on Christians and Jews as their brothers and sisters in Christ — all children of a common Father. The pope was loved and respected. Of those mourning his death in 1958, Jews — who credited Pius XII with being one of their greatest defenders and benefactors in their hour of greatest need — stood in the forefront.

As the public record attests, Pius XII brought to the service of the church and of humanity his deep commitment to the poor, the sick, and the afflicted, and to those especially who suffered because of the Second World War and the ideologies that provoked it.

In a discourse given in Jerusalem, Pope Paul VI stated (January 5, 1964): "We nurture only benevolent thoughts toward all peoples, as did Our predecessor Pius XII, sentiments that he manifested at various times during the world conflict, something that all have been able to witness and above all those who have been helped by him."

On November 18, 1965, Paul VI announced in the Basilica of St. Peter that the Causes of Beatification and Canonization of his predecessors, Pope Pius XII and Pope John XXIII would be initiated. When questioned about the status of

Pius XII's beatification, Reverend Peter Gumpel, SJ, stated: "He was an extraordinary man who faced terrible situations with courage and great wisdom, and who was in his personal life an exemplary Christian, Priest, Bishop, Cardinal, and Pope."

Four

Media Reports

"Nevertheless God holds the Jews most dear for the sake of their Fathers; He does not repent of the gifts He makes or of the calls He issues — such is the witness of the Apostle." — *Nostra Aetate*, Vatican II

The Jewish Press

When Cardinal Eugenio Pacelli was elected pope on March 2, 1939, the Jerusalem *Palestine Post* editorial of March 6, 1939, stated: "Pius XII has clearly shown that he intends to carry on the late Pope's [Pius XI] work for freedom and peace.... We remember that he must have had a large part to play in the recent papal opposition to pernicious race theories and certain aspects of totalitarianism."

The *Jewish Chronicle* in London stated on March 10, 1939, that the Vatican received congratulatory messages from "the Anglo-Jewish Community, the Synagogue Council of America, the Canadian Jewish Congress, and the Polish Rabbinical Council." It also quoted an anti-Nazi speech Cardinal Pacelli delivered in Lourdes in April 1935, and the statements against him in the Nazi *Völkischer Beobachter,* January 22, 1939, with pictures of him and other church dignitaries beneath the heading: "Agitators in the Vatican against Fascism and National Socialism."

The London *Zionist Review* reacted favorably on March 16, 1939, to the appointment of Cardinal Luigi Maglione as secretary of state: "This confirms the view that the new Pope means to conduct an anti-Nazi and anti-Fascist policy."

Jews considered the pope a friend of democracy and peace and an enemy of racism and totalitarianism. With the issuance of Pius XII's first encyclical, the *Jewish Telegraphic Agency* in New York reported on October 27, 1939, that "the unqualified condemnation which Pope Pius XII heaped on totalitarian, racist and materialistic theories of government in his encyclical *Summi Pontificatus* caused a profound stir.... Few observers had expected so outspoken a document."

The editorial on November 9, 1939, of the *American Israelite* in Cincinnati, speaking about the fundamental equality of men, said: "This concept of democracy is reiterated in the Pope's encyclical, stressing again the inviolability of the human person as a sacred being...."

On January 26, 1940, the *Jewish Advocate* in Boston reported: "The Vatican Radio this week broadcast an outspoken denunciation of German atrocities in Nazi [occupied] Poland, declaring they affronted the moral conscience of mankind." This broadcast confirmed media reports about Nazi atrocities, previously dismissed as Allied propaganda.

The general opinion of Jews in the years during and immediately following the war was one of praise and gratitude toward Pope Pius XII. Jews around the world concluded that Pius XII's public statements were directed against the Nazis. They knew that Catholics in the Nazi-occupied and Axis countries were trying to save Jewish lives.

Newspaper Articles

The published correspondence that follows is but a small sample of the immense support the author has received in the continuing struggle for truth about Pius XII.

From Ronald J. Rychlak, "Sister Margherita Marchione's Crusade for Truth," *Catholic Response* (July–August 2007)

Beginning in the 1960s, and continuing to this very day, critics of the Catholic Church have focused on Pius XII, the last pre-Vatican II pope. They have charged Pius with being pro-Nazi, afraid of Hitler, oblivious to what was going on around him, a control freak who was concerned only about a strong papacy.

Many of these charges are inconsistent with one another, but that does not matter to the critics. Their target never really was Pius. At the end of John Cornwell's book *Hitler's Pope*, we learn that the real target was Pope John Paul II. At the end of James Carroll's book *Constantine's Sword*, we learn that he wants to convene Vatican III so that the church can revise the New Testament (as well as all of the church's teachings on sexuality). Daniel Goldhagen, in *A Moral Reckoning*, follows both Cornwell and Carroll but also demands that the Catholic Church pay monetary damages for the harm it has done to Jewish people over the centuries *because it has taught the New Testament!*

The importance of the author's extensive writings and research was recently highlighted when a difference of opinion over Pius XII's efforts nearly created a significant diplomatic problem between the Holy See and the nation of Israel. The matter centered on Israel's Holocaust History Museum, which contains displays where people can learn more about the Nazi efforts to eliminate the Jews. Unfortunately, the museum has a pictorial display of Pope Pius XII alongside photos of Fascist dictators. Under the pope's photograph is an extended caption that says: "Even when reports about the murder of Jews reached the Vatican, the pope did not protest." It continues: "The pope maintained his neutral position throughout the war, with the exception of appeals to the rulers of Hungary and Slovakia toward its end. His silence and the absence of guidelines obliged churchmen throughout Europe to decide on their own how to react."

In reality, few if any individuals did more to support the Jews during this time than did Pope Pius XII. In 2005, shortly after the display went up at the museum, the Holy See's nuncio (ambassador) to Israel wrote a letter asking that it be removed or that the caption be revised. The museum, however, took no action.

The diplomatic issue arose in 2007 when Israel's annual Holocaust Memorial day event was scheduled to take place at the museum. This is a major event, and foreign diplomats are expected to be in attendance. The Vatican's representative, Archbishop Antonio Franco, however, said that he would not attend unless the Pius XII display was changed. "I have my responsibility as a person, a Christian, and representative of the Pope. It is difficult for me, as papal representative, to read this judgment that is not historical and is not true." He told the *Jerusalem Post* that he would "attend any ceremony on the victims of World War II, but I do not feel at ease [in the museum] when the Pope is presented in this way."

This diplomatic standoff made headlines in Israel and was noted around the globe. Fortunately, the problem was resolved when, at the last moment, the museum's director agreed to examine any "new documentation" pertaining to Pius XII and promised to "make sure that we are firmly rooted in the most updated historical truth." If he carries through with that promise, the museum will undoubtedly turn to materials that the author has unearthed and preserved for history. It will also have to change the display.

The research shows us a pope and a Catholic hierarchy deeply involved in a great humanitarian mission to provide help to those in need, irrespective of race, color, or creed. It shows that over the course of the war, the Vatican received nearly 20 million requests for assistance from family members and friends of POWs and missing persons. Pius XII formed the Vatican Information Office to respond to these pleas, and it did an incredible job. Separated families were often put in contact. Other times, travel or accommodations were arranged. Military personnel, civilians, and other victims of war were provided both spiritual and material assistance.

The author's recent book *Crusade of Charity* reprints letters seeking help as well as information as to the Vatican's response. Of course, not all inquires led to happy answers, but this tribute from an elderly grandmother is typical of many letters of thanks received by the Vatican: "With great joy I received the good news about my dear family, my beloved nephews, after a year of silence and anxiety, that only a mother and grandmother can possibly imagine. To whom am I indebted? To the most worthy and most charitable Head of the Church."

Those who follow the news out of Rome know that recently Cardinal Secretary of State Bertone publicly revealed that in October 1943 Pope Pius sent out secret instructions to Catholic institutions informing them of their duty to shelter Jews from the Nazis. This news made headlines in Europe, but to those who have read any of Sister Marchione's books, this was no surprise. She has interviewed literally dozens of witnesses who had firsthand knowledge of this and other, similar instructions from the pope.

Adapted from Lorraine Ash, "A Pope's Determined Defender," *Morris County Daily Record,* May 31, 2007

Did Pope Pius XII Help the Jews? places the eighty-five-year-old scholar in the middle of a world controversy about the late pontiff that affects Jewish/Catholic relations today. From her office and library at Villa Walsh in Morristown, Sister Margherita Marchione pounded out a work the Vatican called "important and timely."

"When I get angry," said the five-foot nun, "I can produce very fast."

What incited her is the text below a picture of Pius XII at Yad Vashem, the holocaust museum in Jerusalem. It states the late pontiff, who reigned during the Holocaust, recognized the Nazi regime and put aside an anti-Semitic encyclical prepared by his predecessor. . . .

Employing the experience of a doctorate and decades as a professor and author, she wrote in her new book that Pius XII did put aside an anti-racist encyclical Jesuits had written for Pius XI. But he did so to pen his own — *Summi Pontificatus,* issued in October 1939. It condemned Nazism and totalitarianism. "His official statements had violent repercussions, though," Sister Marchione said. "The Nazis retaliated and Jews and Catholics in concentration camps suffered more. He determined the Church could do more good by acting quietly."

But quiet does not mean silent. Pius XII saved almost a million Jews by authorizing false baptismal certificates, ordering convents and monasteries to hide Jews, and distributing visas so Jews could enter other countries, according to Sister Marchione....

Gary Krupp, the Jewish founder and president of Pave the Way Foundation, said Sister Marchione's book places historic facts over personal bias. "I challenge any legitimate historic entity to prove any of the well-researched documented statements of this book to be false," said Krupp, whose foundation is dedicated to improving relations between Jews and Catholics.

Though it will be another fifty years before the 6 million documents of Pius XII's reign will be fully archived, Sister Marchione believes there is enough evidence to canonize him since thirty cardinals and bishops recommended that Pope Benedict XVI declare Pius XII "venerable." This is a step on the road to sainthood. But the National Anti-Defamation League urged that action be suspended until archiving is complete.

The issue also is personal to Sister Marchione, who was raised on a Little Ferry farm by Italian immigrant parents and joined the Religious Teachers Filippini at the age of thirteen. The Catholic Church cared for 5,000 Jews in convents and monasteries in 1943 and 1944. Her order cared for 114 Jews. They also helped type responses to 20 million letters requesting help from the Holy Father and the Vatican during the war years. Sister Margherita Marchione remains ready to continue the crusade as long as she has a pen.

Taken from Joan Ruddiman, "Pope Pius XII and the POWs," *Princeton Packet,* **November 10, 2006**

Margherita Marchione, a sister with the Religious Teachers Filippini, breaks every mold her heritage, calling, and age might suggest.... At age 86, she travels the world, promoting the story, backed by credible research, of the role Pope Pius XII played in promoting social justice in an age of terrible darkness. In what Sister Margherita sees as revisionist history, Pope Pius has been "defamed" by those who harbor ill will to the Catholic Church or who have not studied the historical record that supports the wartime pontiff's extraordinary efforts on behalf of Jews.

She has several titles in print on the subject of Pope Pius, including the biography *Pope Pius XII, Architect for Peace.* Two books tackle head-on the history of the Holocaust in Roman Catholic Italy and the pope's role. *Consensus and Controversy: Defending Pope Pius XII* and *Yours Is a Precious Witness: Memoirs of Jews and Catholics in Wartime Italy* make a strong case for the pro-active role the Vatican and Italians took to save the Jews. Even in her autobiography, *The Fighting Nun: My Story,* she devotes a chapter to setting the record straight....

The British historian John Cornwell claims that the pope's silence during the Holocaust condemned thousands of Jews to death by the Nazis. He further argues that Pius cut deals with Hitler in order to save German Catholics from persecution by the Nazis. Ultimately, Cornwell condemns Pope Pius as an anti-Semite who was a willing agent to Hitler's master plan.

In person and in her writing, she builds a dramatic counter-argument based on extensive research, most of it primary documents, diaries, and interviews of firsthand accounts from Italian lay people, religious and Jews. She has faced off with Cornwell on several occasions on radio and television programs and has successfully faced him down. *Hitler's Pope: The Secret History of Pius II* (1999) by John Cornwell is an outrageous book that not only distorts the truth about the extraordinary efforts of Pius XII and the church to save the Jews, but actually also depicts this saintly pope as a collaborator of the Nazis. This is revisionist history. There is a need to set the record straight. . . .

Sister Margherita explores the historical context in order to understand the historic record. Was Pope Pius silent? No, actually he spoke out officially on several occasions against Hitler and the actions of Nazi Germany. Sister Margherita provides photos of those official documents and newspaper accounts of the Vatican's official actions. Moreover, she connects the historical dots by providing the chronology of those official statements and the violent repercussions in Germany and in Poland to Catholics, including nuns and priests. In Dachau in Poland alone, twenty-eight hundred priests were imprisoned. More than half died there.

Pope Pius determined that the church, and Rome, could do more good by acting subversively rather than speaking officially against Hitler. To that end, convents, monasteries, even the Vatican itself, on the pope's orders, were opened as havens for Jews. One amazing photograph in Sister Margherita's collection shows a dozen young Jewish mothers holding their infants in what is captioned "the Nursery." Sister Margherita points out that the tapestry visible in the background has the pope's seal. The pope gave up his private quarters to house these women and their babies.

As a Religious Teacher Filippini, Sister Margherita has access to the sisters of her order in Italy who participated in the sheltering of Jews. They share stories of setting up their cots throughout the convents, including the basements, so Jewish families could have the small bedrooms. The priests and nuns had other special resources besides spacious buildings with a lot of rooms. Of critical importance, they maintained quantities of food for their own large populations and therefore did not raise suspicions when shopping for large orders. Moreover, she notes, "these people could take risks because they had no dependents." However, the religious were not immune to suspicion and arrest. She writes, "Those sent to prison were treated with brutality and contempt. Many were killed in reprisal for helping anti-Fascists and Jews."

Rather than being a "handmaiden to Hitler," according to Sister Margherita, the record shows that the pontiff was cleverly subversive in sheltering Jews as he protected the church against Nazi forces.

Now in her book *Crusade of Charity: Pope Pius XII and POWs, 1939–1945* (2006) Sister Margherita tells the story of the Vatican Information Office, which brought relief to war victims....

Fordham University historian Oskar Halecki wrote in 1951, "One of the Pope's most remarkable achievements during the war was the successful establishment of the Vatican Information Office, a feat which ranks favorably with any similar military or diplomatic undertaking."

The evidence is overwhelming. Sister Margherita maintains a steady drumbeat of facts and support from esteemed diplomats and historians to squelch any suggestion that the Vatican, as directed by Pope Pius XII, was not actively working daily to "mitigate the effects of wars he could not prevent."

Sister Margherita captures the chaos and confusion of a war-torn world and the abject despair of mothers, wives, soldiers, and children of all races and religions who reached out to the Vatican for help. In one passage, she explains how Vatican Radio was used to contact prisoners of war.

"Names were spelled out letter by letter to avoid misunderstandings. The letter of each name was given the initial of famous Italian cities, since it was possible neither to repeat nor to clarify a conversation. This is how names, regardless of race or religion, were announced in response to the sighs and prayers of countless grieving mothers and wives. Indeed, Vatican Radio's service for tracing missing persons, both civil and military, helped compensate for the lack of normal communication." ...

Not only Sister Margherita but also other reputable historians, including Martin Gilbert in *Never Again: The History of the Holocaust,* are seriously questioning the caliber of historical research done by Cornwell and others who suggest that Pope Pius worked in collusion with Hitler. Sheer numbers alone dispute the critics; Italy stands with Denmark in saving the greatest number of Jews from the Holocaust.

For those who wonder about the role the Catholic Church played during the war, and if the innuendo about "Hitler's Pope" could have some basis in fact, once again Sister Margherita provides ample evidence that good works were being done by the pope and all his minions — within the ranks of the religious as well as faithful Catholics throughout Italy. Thousands of Jewish lives were saved and, now the record shows, hundreds of thousands more of all races and religions were aided by the efforts of the Vatican Information Office as established by Pope Pius XII. He was, Sister Margherita says, "a man of extraordinary charity."

From "Yad Vashem's Mind Made Up about Pius XII: Don't Confuse Them with Facts!" *Annotico Report*, June 4, 2007

Despite the mounting evidence that Pius XII contributed more to the saving of Holocaust Jews than did American Jews, Estee Yaari, spokesperson for Yad Vashem, claims that Sister Margherita's correspondence to the museum is on file there, though the museum considers the text on its panel about Pius XII "an accurate summary of the historical documentation at our disposal."

Yaari speaks only about Sister Margherita's correspondence and says nothing about her book *Did Pope Pius XII Help the Jews?* (2007). Neither does he address *The Myth of Hitler's Pope: How Pope Pius XII Rescued Jews from the Nazis* (2005) by Rabbi David G. Dalin, or *Righteous Gentiles: How Pius XII and the Catholic Church Saved Half a Million Jews from the Nazis* (2005) by Mississippi law professor Ronald Rychlak.

Nor does Yad Vashem acknowledge any merit to the religion editor of *Newsweek*, Kenneth L. Woodward, who summarizes *Hitler's Pope* as having "errors of fact and ignorance of context [that] appear on almost every page." More recently, John Cornwell acknowledged that he erred in many ways when writing *Hitler's Pope*. Yaari does not comment on *A Special Mission: Hitler's Secret Plot to Seize the Vatican and Kidnap Pope Pius XII* (2007) by Dan Kurzman, referring to a plot hatched because Hitler considered Pius XII "the Jews' Pope."

"One writer submitted questions that need to be answered: What are the Pope's priorities? Should the Vatican be passing judgment on other religions? What is it that the Jewish

Community claims the Pope should have done or that he did not do? What were the shortcomings in the Jewish leadership during the Holocaust? Should the ADL not be concerned with the persecution of others by Israelis?"

The record shows that Eugenio Pacelli as secretary of state and as pope openly and consistently defied the Nazis and encouraged the German bishops to continue to do so. During the Nazi occupation of Rome, from September 1943 to June 1944, Pius XII made strong protests against the Nazi seizure of Rome's Jews and took decisive action to protect them. He permitted false documents, forged protective passes, and faked baptismal certificates to be issued in order to save as many Jewish lives as possible. The extraordinary tributes the Jewish community offered Pius XII for saving Jews and fighting anti-Semitism is part of world history.

With so much available documentation, it is incredible that the debate concerning the actions of Pius XII has not terminated. The publication of an essential new book, *Did Pope Pius XII Help the Jews?* (2007)...will contribute to the future termination of that debate, at which time Pius XII will be rightly honored by the world as a hero, a saint, and a "Righteous Gentile."

Misrepresentations and Testimonials

Bill Loughlin, unpublished "Letter to the Editor," *Tidings*

One may well ask has anybody written a book favorable to Pius XII and the Catholic Church during Word War II? The correct answer is yes, and it is to its everlasting credit that some have been reviewed in the *Tidings*.

Unfortunately, because of its "official silence" those authors and their books have received virtually no recognition in the pages of the *Los Angeles Times*. As a result the general public has been left with little other than what one national Catholic magazine several years ago described as the "libel that lasts."

The necessity for penetrating the walls of secular silence as to the truth of the wartime contributions of Pius XII and the Vatican becomes painfully obvious when considering the results of the accepted revisionism that has persisted to date.

In a news story of March 13, 2000, on "Teaching about the Holocaust," the *Times* reported that "students have faced such tough questions as why did the church remain silent while 6 million Jews were put to death?" The obvious assumption foisted on the kids is that the church did, in fact, remain silent. That's rather strange, to put it politely, given the fact that the public record during the war years, let alone the archival material from Nazi sources since then, clearly indicates that Pius was anything but silent. Unfortunately, as the *Times* itself noted, the result of such teaching is that some students were prompted to "question their faith in the church."

Sister Margherita presented a more recent example of the damage done. In an article June 24, 2007, in the *National Catholic Register,* she reported receiving a letter from a distraught mother who accompanied her eighth-grade daughter on a class field trip to the Museum of Tolerance in Los Angeles. The woman said she was "shocked and offended" by a film portraying the pope and the Vatican as having done nothing on behalf of the Jews. When she volunteered to tell the class some stories about Catholics rescuing the Jews and what Pius did, the woman was denied permission by the principal and the parish priest who said, "I could not present this information because the church says that Pope Pius XII and the Catholic Church were just bystanders."

We hear a lot these days about accountability in the field of politics. The time has come for Catholic educators to find a cure for the incalculable damage such cockeyed propaganda is having on their young charges.

Margherita Marchione, Letter to the Editor, *Morris County Daily Record*, May 6, 2000

In his letter of May 3, 2000, Ed Rosen does not provide evidence for his allegations about Pope Pius XII. The historical record shows that as nuncio in Germany, Cardinal Pacelli spoke out repeatedly against Nazism. He later became Vatican secretary of state and negotiated a Concordat with the Germans in 1933, in order to protect the rights of Catholics. The truth is that the church did not terminate the Catholic Party. The Vatican agreed to the Concordat only after Hitler's reign of terror forced the Party to dissolve itself. While priests and religious were not to engage in party politics (This is still church policy!), it did not impede political and social activities on the part of lay Catholics. Pius XII always singled out Hitler and the Nazis as the worst danger for Germany and the world. He did everything in his power to preserve Germany's Catholic Center Party.

Elected pope on March 2, 1939, Pius XII continued to support German Catholics. He exhorted his representatives to oppose the racial laws and to intervene on behalf of persecuted Jews. The Nazi press accused him of being anti-German, and the International Communist newspaper called him a "relentless opponent of Hitler!"

Pius XII assisted Jews in leaving Germany and spoke out frequently and consistently. He even appealed to the United

States to throw open its doors to Jewish refugees, but his request was unsuccessful. Throughout the 1930s, everyone understood Pius XII's opposition to anti-Semitism.

Margherita Marchione, "An Analysis of the Distortion," 2005

The January 9, 2005, *New York Times* article by Elaine Sciolino and Jason Horowitz is misleading and has misrepresented the facts. It presents a distorted analysis of the position of the Catholic Church with regard to the Jewish children saved during World War II. It quotes from a document, which may be a fraud, in an article by Alberto Melloni that appeared recently (December 28, 2004) in the *Corriere della Sera,* an Italian anticlerical newspaper. One questions the authenticity of the document. It appears suspicious. There is no validity to its claims. It is simply a new attack on Pius XII, whose courage and charity toward Jews has been documented.

The alleged document was not written by Pius XII: the handwriting is unknown, it has no signature, it is not written on official Vatican stationery, it is incomplete, it is written in French (ordinarily such documents from the Vatican to the nuncios were in Italian), and the researcher wishes to remain anonymous. But why the secrecy?

The claim that Jewish children who were baptized should not be returned to their parents is outrageous. There is absolutely no indication that these so-called instructions to Nuncio Angelo Roncalli (later Pope John XXIII) came from Pius XII.

There is no evidence that Pius XII ever ordered anyone not to hand over a Jewish child to its rightful parents. In fact, in his book *Avenue of the Righteous* (1980), Peter Hellman writes about a Polish Catholic woman who was unwilling to return a Jewish girl to her father. The woman, who was raising the child as a Catholic, sought the pope's permission to keep her. Peter Hellman reports: "She was instructed by the Pope to return the child to its father."

The policy of the Catholic Church was to save these children who would have been sent to concentration camps and exterminated. In general these children were educated and returned to their parents or relatives. I interviewed Jews who confirmed the fact that, as children hidden in convents, their religion was respected. Many remained orphans, and the church provided for their future. Some requested baptism. Canon Law required that a baptized child receive adequate instruction in the faith....

Testimonials of Jewish survivors of the Holocaust also make it perfectly clear that the pope was not anti-Semitic or indifferent to the fate of the Jews, and that he did everything possible to help them. In a letter dated August 8, 2004, historian and Holocaust survivor Michael Tagliacozzo wrote: "Any apology for the actions of Pius XII must be considered superfluous. This is clear to all men of good will and is entrusted above all to the memory of those Jews, now living, who have not forgotten the efforts and solicitude of Pope Pacelli...."

Regarding the shameful campaign of defamation, Tagliacozzo writes: "To refute this injustice, it suffices to recall the precious testimonials of Jews who lived during that tragic period of history. Among those thanking the Pope in 1943 were Israeli soldiers who came from Palestine; Chief Rabbi Isaac Herzog; David Ben Gurion, head of the Israeli government; Golda Meir, foreign minister; the three rabbis of Rome, Israel Zolli, David Prato, and Elio Toaff; Gideon Hausner, procurator general of the State of Israel; Nahum Goldmann, president of the World Jewish Congress.

"To these one must add the countless expressions of gratitude of those whose lives were saved in the religious houses in Rome, Assisi, and elsewhere. Even if gratitude was expressed directly to the Institutions that protected them, the merit goes to Pope Pacelli who, on October 16, 1943, gave orders to open the doors of the parishes, convents, and monasteries to save the Jews from deportation."

... Researchers should consult the articles about Pius XII and the Catholic Church printed in the *New York Times* during and after World War II.... Professor Pietro DeMarco concludes that this lack of clarity has harmed the relations between the church and the Jewish world.

Radio Broadcasts

Catholic University of America Protests

The broadcast "Catholic Protest against Nazis," made on November 16, 1938, occurred prior to Germany's invasion of Poland and three years before the United States would enter World War II. It was a live national broadcast from the CUA campus that was carried by both CBS and NBC.

The first speaker was Reverend Maurice S. Sheeley, head of the Department of Religious Education, whose words set the tone: "The world is witnessing a great tragedy in Europe today, and after sober, calm reflection, various groups and leaders of the Catholic Church have sought permission to raise their voices, not in mad hysteria, but in firm indignation against the atrocities visited upon Jews in Germany."

During the twenty-seven-minute broadcast, the university's chief executive, Monsignor Joseph M. Corrigan, remarked that this was "a persecution hardly if ever equaled since earlier blood-lusting paganism martyred Christians for their faith in God."

Archbishop John J. Mitty of San Francisco and Bishop Peter L. Ireton of Richmond, Virginia, declared their solidarity with Jewish people. Bishop John M. Gannon of Erie, Pennsylvania, stated: "In the face of such injustice toward the Jews of Germany, I express my revulsion, disgust, and grief." Former governor of New York Al Smith asked if Germany had fallen into the hands of a band of ruffians. The speakers all expressed Catholic moral outrage on behalf of the Jews.

An article in the Fall 2007 issue of the *Catholic University of America Magazine* includes newspaper headlines that describe the broadcast's impact: "Prominent Churchmen Denounce Oppression of Jews by Germans," "Catholic Churchmen Join Pleas for Jews," "Noted Layman, Clerics Voice Nazi Protest." This live national broadcast from the CUA campus was heard around the nation.

The Catholic University's response was among the many responses that American Catholics made to *Kristallnacht* and to the persecution of Germany's Jews. Perhaps Holocaust museums around the world will now include this "early outpouring of solidarity that flowed from American Catholics to their German Jewish brothers and sisters — a welcome addition to the pages of history."[1]

---

1. See *http://libraries.cua.edu/achrcua/antinazi.html* to listen to a clip or read a transcript of the 1938 broadcast.

Pacelli was ordained a priest on April 2, 1899, and celebrated his first Mass in the Basilica of Saint Mary Major.

Pope Pius XII speaks from the papal throne.

Pope Pius XII walking in the Vatican Gardens while preparing his talks.

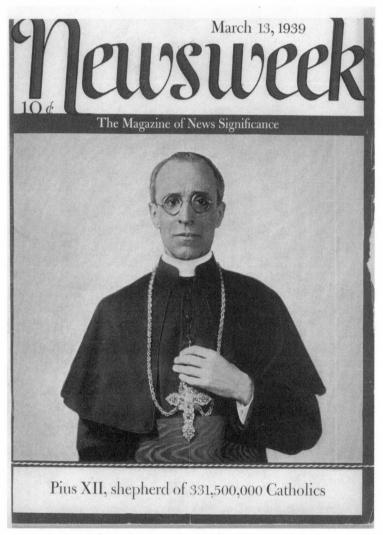

March 13, 1939

Newsweek

10¢

The Magazine of News Significance

Pius XII, shepherd of 331,500,000 Catholics

Pope Pius XII appears on the cover of *Newsweek* in March 1939.

Pope Pius XII addressing the crowd after the bombing of Rome on July 19, 1943.

Refugees, mostly women and children, make a home in the papal
apartments at Castelgandolfo.

Papal Nuncio Eugenio Pacelli assists in handing out blankets
to the homeless and refugees.

"VATICANO" is clearly visible on the side of a truck assigned to the transportation of refugees.

Vatican trucks prepare for distribution of food to refugees in Rome.

Rome was liberated on June 5, 1944. A huge demonstration was held as the people honored Papa Pacelli for having saved Rome from total destruction.

Pius XII greets American pilots.

In gratitude for having saved so many Jews, on May 26, 1955,
the Israeli Philharmonic performed Beethoven's Seventh Symphony
in the presence of Pius XII.

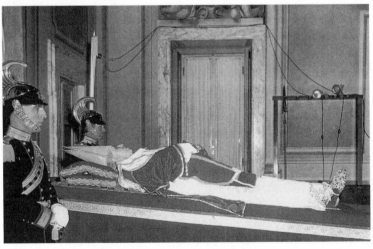

His remains were first viewed in Castelgandolfo.

Pope Benedict XVI praying before the tomb of Pope Pius XII.

Vatican stamp
of Pope Pius XII.

An Agentinean commemorative
stamp in honor of Pope Pius XII.

Five

Personal Encounters

Whoever saves one life... it is as though he had saved the whole world. — Sanhedrin IV, 5

World War II began six months after Pius XII was elected on March 2, 1939. Throughout this period, fear of reprisals was an element in Vatican diplomatic policy. But Pope Pius XII was not fearful. For thirteen years Eugenio Pacelli had been in Germany as papal nuncio and was outspoken against the Nazis. In recent years, some Jewish organizations object strongly to the statement that Pope Pius XII personally or through his representatives contributed to saving hundreds of thousands of Jewish lives. They claim he did not do enough when in fact he did more than all the other world leaders combined.

No one can deny the historical record, which shows that Pope Pius XII, through his worldwide network of apostolic delegates, was able to save the lives of thousands of Jews during the Holocaust. He did all he could to avoid reprisals against Jews and Catholics. As the spiritual leader of all, including 40 million German Catholics, he could not endanger them. It is foolish to think that the assistance given Jews in the Vatican and in Rome would have been successful without his knowledge and protection.

Eyewitness Reports

To protect and assist the Jews during the Nazi years meant that the lives of entire Christian families and religious men and women would be endangered. Many were detained and sent to concentration camps after Jews were found hidden in their homes.

In a letter to the editor of *La Repubblica* (April 27, 1986), Ines Gistron wrote: "I was placed with my Jewish friend in a *pensione* run by Canadian nuns at Monteverde (Rome). We were given false IDs. We lived with elderly women and young ladies, completely separated from the nuns in the cloister. After the Nazis began searching for Jews, the *pensione* was so filled that the Holy Father ordered the cloistered areas to be opened in order to provide for more refugees. I gave my room to a woman with two children and went to live in a very small cell. . . . Because of Pius XII's prudence, did he not succeed in saving many lives, including mine?"

An important witness to the role of Pius XII in wartime Italy is Israel Zolli, chief rabbi of Rome during the Nazi occupation and persecution of Jews. In his book *Antisemitismo,* he states: "World Jewry owes a great debt of gratitude to Pius XII for his repeated and pressing appeals for justice on behalf of the Jews and, when these did not prevail, for his strong protests against evil laws and procedures."

Papal Directives

The following documents provide abundant evidence of papal directives to church institutions to shelter Jews. The first account was written on September 26, 2000: "I, Sister Domenica Mitaritonna, declare under oath that during the period of the war 1942–1943, I was living at Via Caboto, 16, Rome, and assisted two or three Jewish families who sought refuge in our convent. They were welcomed with immense hospitality by the Superior who had been solicited by the Vatican to help them." All were saved. In fact, the Sisters received official recognition from the Jewish community of Rome "recalling how they risked their lives to save Jews from Nazi-Fascist atrocities."

During my trip to Rome in November 2006, I met with twenty-five Jews who wished to place a plaque on the Via Botteghe Oscure Convent of the Religious Teachers Filippini, where their relatives (a group of sixty Jews) had been saved during the Nazi occupation of Rome. These Jews gave me notarized statements and acknowledged the fact that the Sisters followed the instructions of Pope Pius XII.

A journal entry dated June 5, 1944, states: "Today began the exodus of the Jewish refugees. Over sixty women and children occupied the area designated for students, and also several rooms in the convent." A similar entry recorded on June 8, 1944, notes that, following Vatican directives, these Sisters sponsored the "opening of a soup kitchen where the Sisters served meals to all refugees." These Sisters assisted Pius XII in caring for innocent civilians and racial groups targeted by Nazi persecution.

On October 18, 1943, just two days after the Nazi roundup of Rome's Jews, a firsthand observer, Madame de Wyss, wrote in her Roman diary that "the Jews have implored help from the pope, and that Pius XII has asked the German Ambassador Weizsäcker to stop this ill-treatment and violence." A few days later (October 24), Robert Hale wrote, "Jews are still persecuted, though less...because, it is said, the pope intervened on their behalf."

Additional Support

After World War II, Cardinal Pietro Palazzini and Italian historian Renzo De Felice researched the number of Jewish guests in 155 convents and monasteries throughout Rome. Although their research has been reported,[1] Pius XII's detractors have not recognized the extraordinary action taken by the pope and others, anxious to carry out his express wish that those being pursued by the Nazis be helped in every way possible.

Cardinal Ersilio Tonini of Ravenna has effectively summed up the case against Pius's critics: "When he had to speak out, the Pope was not afraid. He condemned Hitler's invasion of Belgium, defining it as a crime against every human and divine right. In Rome he ordered that the doors of all buildings belonging to the Vatican be opened for Jews and other political refugees. When Jewish students were forbidden by Fascist law to continue their studies, the Pope arranged for the pontifical universities to accept them."

Now that Pius's cause for canonization is being vociferously opposed by Abraham Foxman of the Anti-Defamation League, it is imperative that the essential facts concerning the wartime pope's help for Jews be set emphatically before the general public. Anyone who would belittle the assistance that Pius gave the Jews must also reject the current scholarship along with the works of a score of careful researchers including the editors of the twelve-volume *Actes* (1965–82).

In addition, it is crucial that the extraordinary testimony of others be given serious consideration: The record shows that over fifty refugees were saved in the Vatican Pontifical College for Priests. Their names were compiled by Cardinal Pietro

---

1. See the appendix in Marchione, *Yours Is a Precious Witness: Memoirs of Jews and Catholics in Wartime Italy* (1997).

Palazzini in 1995. He also compiled the names of the refugees who were in the Vatican Pontifical Seminary. Here there are over two hundred names and each name is followed by a description (Professor, Student, Ambassador, Military, etc.).

In 1963, Professor Renzo De Felice compiled a list of the institutions in Rome with the number of Jewish refugees in each convent or monastery: 109 had between 1 and 32; 36 had between 33 and 96; 10 had between 100 and 400. Professor De Felice calculated 114 refugees staying in three of the convents belonging to the Religious Teachers Filippini in Rome.

There are the many testimonials in the files of religious orders in Rome and elsewhere in Italy. As a typical example, consider the records of my own order, the Religious Teachers Filippini. I interviewed Sister Ida Greco, who signed the following testimonial on July 30, 2007: "I, Sister Ida Greco, was a resident at Via Botteghe Oscure, 42, during the Nazi occupation of Rome. I can confirm that in those days we knew that the Holy Father had given orders to all superiors to open the doors of convents and monasteries to all Jews and other refugees. I remember that I helped prepare meals and that I was there when the Vatican sent us food to help feed the 60 Jewish guests."

In the Archives of the Sisters of the Most Precious Blood in Rome, one can read letters of gratitude and thanksgiving written by Jews, for example: "Rome, December 13, 1946: The wedding of my daughter Elsa makes me recall with profound gratitude to you who with such human Charity took care of my women during the sad months of the German occupation, saving them from the dangers of the death camps. I also recall the loving comfort given by the Mother President, and the silent faith of Sister Maria that gave us much hope.

This splendid act of brotherhood deserves to be written in marble with gold letters so that it will never be forgotten. I enclose a small offering [L. 3000] for you to use as you think best.... Adolfo Tabet, via Po, n. 162."

Among other letters there is one dated August 10, 1944, from Enrica Anav Brunetti, Via Bodoni, 6, Rome: "It is with much delay that I fulfill my duty to you and the very kind Sisters. My office schedule does not permit me to come at the proper hour, to extend my greetings and express my most heartfelt thanks for the hospitality given me and my family, during the sad circumstances of the infamous Nazi-Fascist persecutions. Because I am sure of further delay, I am sending you this note to reassure you that I shall never forget the benefits received and to remind you that my gratitude will never diminish. Never will I forget you who have been impressed on my heart. It will be impossible to forget you. Therefore, I beg you to excuse me and to accept the expression of my most devout sentiments toward you and the kind Sisters."

According to an unpublished journal of an Augustinian nun in the convent of Santi Quattro Coronati in Rome, Pius XII instructed the mother superior to allow those fleeing from the Germans to enter the cloistered convent and remain as long as necessary. Not only does the Augustinian author provide details, but she explains that the pope wished to save "the children as well as Jews" and ordered that monasteries and enclosures should be opened to protect those persecuted. She admits she prepared false identity papers for all her guests. "Unfortunately," the nun writes, "with the coming of the Germans in September, the war against the Jews — whom they wish to exterminate with the most barbarous atroci-ties — included young Italians and political activists who were tortured and subjected to the most horrible sufferings.... We adhered to the wishes of the Holy Father."

Other testimonials, dating from October 16, 1943, relate to the acceptance of Jews during the persecution and may be found in many religious communities. I cite one from the Congregation of the Adorers of the Most Precious Blood on Via Pannonia 10, Rome, where entire families of Jews found safe refuge. They lived on the third and fourth floors of a wing designated for the school and they remained there for two full years.

Sister Alma Pia De Rossi wrote to the vicariate of Rome: "From the lists preserved we can state that the number of Jews was 112, not counting the many children hidden with each family." (Renzo De Felice notes that the total number of Jews hidden in this convent was 136.) Among them was the family of Mr. Romeo Bondi, the janitor of the Jewish school on Lungo Tevere Sanzio. These documents state that, "when he knew that his school would be sacked, he wanted to save its contents. He then contacted the Vicariate for help.... Monsignor Gentileschi advised him to bring everything to areas in our school building. This list is preserved here. It is dated December 14, 1943."

Collectively these witnesses demonstrate that the Catholic Church under the direction of Pope Pius XII saved more people from the Nazis and Fascists than any other leader in the world.

Witness to a Miracle

Michael Tagliacozzo, one of the intended victims of Nazi and Fascist madness in Italy, has become a leading scholar of Jewish suffering from 1939 to 1945. His research makes him not only a pivotal historian of the Italian Holocaust but also an expert on the response of Pius XII and the Vatican to the Nazis.

The accuracy of his work is unquestioned. Meir Michaelis, author of the most acclaimed study of the entire Fascist-Nazi period, *Mussolini and the Jews: German-Italian Relations and the Jewish Question in Italy 1922–1945* (1978), called Tagliacozzo "the outstanding expert" on the Jewish situation in Rome during the war.

While the scholarship is praised, his conclusions about Pope Pius XII and the Vatican have often been ignored or circumvented and sometimes twisted to condemn both the pope and the church. It's clear that Tagliacozzo knows more about the pope's attitude toward Jews than the great majority of those passing judgment on the pontiff — including many Catholics, some church leaders, and some claiming to be objective scholars.

If the uncontestable evidence that Tagliacozzo provides were properly weighed, Pius XII would be regarded as one of history's most revered pontiffs. His wisdom, charity, and inspired judgment would have been formally recognized decades ago by the church.

The information contained here is primarily drawn from his notes to me, conversations, and his autobiographical writings. My knowledge is limited mainly to his place in Pius XII studies.

Scenes from a Life

Michael Tagliacozzo is a historian, a Holocaust survivor, a key witness to the actions of Pius, a teacher, and now an elderly truth-seeker much given to the prayerful study of scripture. Born in Rome on December 19, 1921, he is the son of Isacco and Anita Di Veroli. He comes from an ancient Jewish-Roman family, faithfully Jewish but assimilated into the culture of the dominant Italian-Christian environment.

As a teenager, Michael went to a rabbinical school (not a school for rabbis) and a state upper elementary school. He also notes: "Until October 1938, I was part of the 'Italian Youth of Littorio,' which was an organization of the National Fascist Party. Almost all young Italians, Christians and Jews, were required to join the organization." But when the racial laws in 1938 were enacted, he was expelled both from national schools and the Fascist youth organization.

Fortunately, his family found tutors for him, and he continued his studies privately. Five years later, when he was fleeing the Nazis, it would be a tutor, along with Vatican priests and an Evangelical minister, who enabled him to escape the Nazis and Fascists seeking to arrest him. Michael speaks of going with a group of Jewish students to a public audience with Pius XII in St. Peter's Basilica in 1942.

The danger for Jews immensely increased on September 22, 1943, when the Nazis became the military rulers of Rome. Tagliacozzo has written in detail about what their presence meant to him personally.

"Two weeks after the German occupation of Rome, I abandoned my home in the Monteverde Nuovo section in order to avoid service imposed by the Nazis on all Jews born between 1910 and 1922. Various reports had reached us about the anti-Jewish persecution in countries occupied by the Germans. I moved in with a Jewish family in the Nomentana District. The British had landed on the heel of Italy and the Americans in Salerno. We thought they would soon reach Rome, but that did not happen for some time.

"At 6:15 on Saturday morning of October 16, 1943, the third day of the Feast of the Tabernacles, we were still in our beds when some SS burst into our apartment.... While the soldiers were busy checking on who there they could arrest, that is, on who was Jewish, I was able to lower myself from a window and hide in an apartment on the floor below...where a Catholic family lived that I knew by sight. Being able to hide in that apartment and divine assistance saved me. Sadly, the Jewish family I was living with — a widow with a twenty-two-year-old son and a nineteen-year-old daughter — were captured and deported to Auschwitz. I later learned that as soon as they arrived on October 23, the mother and daughter were sent to the gas chamber, while the son endured forced labor in the mines of Silesia and died of exhaustion in February of 1944.

"Desperately looking for a place to hide, I went to the home of Professor Maria Amendola, my literature tutor. She took me in and helped me get in touch with a young priest, Father Vincenzo Fagiolo (later a Cardinal). He, in turn, pointed me toward Monsignor Roberto Ronca, rector of the Pontifical Seminary, in the extraterritorial zone of the Lateran. I immediately went there and remained in the seminary for over three months....

"Then Italian Fascist collaborators, illegally and sacrilegiously, broke into the Basilica of Saint Paul's Outside the Walls on the night and early morning of February 3 and 4, 1944. I, with other refugees hiding in the seminary, fled, fearing a possible invasion of the Lateran area.

"For some 20 days I remained with the Evangelical Pastor Daniele Cupertino of the Church of the Adventists. During that time the only food we had came from Father Pietro Palazzini, who was assisting political and Jewish refugees in the seminary. He generously provided us with food. Next I was taken in by the Franciscan Fathers of the Lateran Penitentiary, where I remained until the liberation of Rome on June 4, 1944."

In a 2007 letter to me Tagliacozzo wrote: "With hope and with God's help and the friendships of kindly Christian brothers, I avoided the cruel October round-up and stayed nine months in the major seminary of the Lateran. In that Catholic environment I was able to witness at close range how Pope Pacelli's paternal solicitude inspired priests and seminarians to serve the persecuted. I strove to repay the debts of gratitude that I owed for my survival. . . . Among other things, I was instrumental in obtaining the Israeli honor of 'Just Among the Nations,' which was awarded to Cardinals Palazzini and Fagiolo" (see *L'Osservatore Romano,* February 28, 1985).

For nearly sixty years Tagliacozzo has been in Israel, his "spiritual" homeland. An essential part of his life there has been to continue his own writing and publishing on the Holocaust and whenever possible to talk with other scholars and teach young students. In the last decade or so both his teaching and research have been connected with the "Beth Lohamé Haghettaot Center" (House of Ghetto Opponents), located in Galilee near the city of St. John of Acri. It consists of a museum, an extensive collection of documents concerning children, a general archive with over a million documents, a library of books in ten languages, an art collection, and a humanistic center for those who want to study the Shoah. The humanistic center's stated purpose is "to inspire ideals of tolerance and equality of a pluralistic society."

Tagliacozzo explains that he has been more or less a volunteer, without financial recompense, working in the center's

Italian section dealing with historical documents of World War II. In all of his undertakings, Tagliacozzo's defense of Pius XII has not been forgotten. If anything, his findings have been restated with more insistence.

Conclusion

The Holocaust was the evil consequence of the demonic mind of Adolf Hitler, who planned to dominate the world and foster a new godless religion. Kenneth L. Woodward wrote in *Newsweek:* "No one person, Hitler excepted, was responsible for the Holocaust. And no one person, Pius XII included, could have prevented it. In choosing diplomacy over protest, Pius XII had his priorities straight. It's time to lay off this pope."

If Pope Pius XII had denounced Adolf Hitler more explicitly, the Nazis would have responded with even more ferocity. Personally and through his representatives, Pius XII employed all the means at his disposal to save Jews and other refugees during World War II. As a moral leader and a diplomat forced to limit his words, he privately took action and, despite insurmountable obstacles, saved thousands of Jews from the gas chambers.

Today this story must be told in order to stop the calumnies against Pius XII and the Catholic Church. True, the church has survived persecutions for two thousand years and continues its mission of evangelization. However, today the anti-Catholicism prevalent in the media and the negative propaganda about Pope Pius XII mislead many Catholics who do not understand the present controversy. Pius XII was not anti-Semitic. He was prudent and did all he could to save

Jews, Catholics, and others whom Hitler wanted to kill. Why have countless eyewitnesses been ignored?

While some individuals, including Jews, betrayed their Jewish friends, the pope saved lives. He did all he could to avoid reprisals against Jews and Catholics. As the spiritual leader of all, including 40 million German Catholics, he could not endanger them. Not only did he provide money, ships, and food, but he placed his radio, his diplomacy, and his convents at the disposal of the refugees. He feared that by publicly condemning Hitler, many more lives would have been destroyed. No one can deny the historical record, which shows that Pope Pius XII, through his worldwide network of apostolic delegates, was able to save the lives of thousands of Jews during the Holocaust.

Six

Additional Information

The Church established by God as the rock of human brotherhood and peace can never come to terms with the idol-worshippers of brutal violence.

— Pope Pius XII, from the
Ten Commandments for Peace

Newly Discovered Documents

Reporter and author Andrea Tornielli includes in his recent work newly discovered documents concerning Pope Pius XII that contain a rich family correspondence and new testimonies found in the *Actes* of the cause for beatification.[1]

These new documents include letters written in the 1920s by Eugenio Pacelli, who was then the apostolic nuncio to Munich, to his brother Francesco Pacelli. In one letter the future pope expresses his great anxiety about the origin and activities of the Nazi party, which proves false the opinion that Pius XII was in favor of Nazism. It also reveals the fact that Pacelli did not want to make a career in the Roman Curia and become a cardinal; he preferred a pastoral ministry as bishop in one of the Italian dioceses.

---

1. Andrea Tornielli, *Pio XII: Eugenio Pacelli: Un uomo sul trono di Pietro* (2007).

In much of the correspondence with his brother, Eugenio confides many personal details about his requests to the Vatican secretary of state that were not heeded. For example, while Eugenio Pacelli tried to reach an agreement between the church and Bavaria, Secretary of State Gasparri instead preferred one with all Germany, which, at the time, was composed of seventeen different states. The unpublished letters describe the differences of opinion between Pacelli and the Vatican. He writes to Gasparri: "Since the Superiors have not accepted my respectful request with regard to not sending me the 'Uditore,' it remains for me to simply obey."

For decades Pacelli confronted world problems. On June 22, 1920, he became the first apostolic nuncio to Germany. Four years later, March 29, 1924, he signed a concordat with Bavaria, which was ratified by its Parliament on January 15, 1925. It determined the rights and duties of the church and the government in respect to each other. After concluding a concordat with Bavaria, Pacelli was able to succeed with Prussia and Baden, but had no success with either the Reich or the Soviet Union. After some time in Munich, the apostolic nuncio's residence was transferred to Berlin. His peace efforts did not succeed. The Germans were not ready for peace.

Regardless of his private convictions, Pacelli saw republicanism as good for Germany. An incident demonstrating Pacelli's support for a democratic-republican government took place in Munich in 1922. At a hostile political meeting, Konrad Adenauer, who later became chancellor of the West German Republic, defended republicanism as the best hope for Germany. His audience favored the Kaiser. When Adenauer finished his speech and Cardinal Michael von Faulhaber rose for a rebuttal of Adenauer's arguments, Pacelli jerked at Faulhaber's cassock. The cardinal was surprised but he sat down and went along with the diplomatic intuitions of the papal nuncio.

This seems to preview his support for democracy rooted in the laws of God as outlined in his 1944 Christmas address and demonstrated later by his encouragement of the Christian Democrats in Italy after World War II.

There is no difference between reports to the Vatican secretary of state and the information he reveals in his letters to his brother Francesco. In no way did Pacelli distance himself from his position with regard to anti-Semitism. Furthermore, his sentiments are no different from those expressed in his official dispatches to the Vatican. In April 1924 he writes: "In general, the entire situation is very difficult in Germany because of the progress made by the nationalist parties which are fanatically anti-Catholic." In the light of this documentation, the black legend depicting the future Pope Pius XII as pro-Nazi appears unfounded.

The Lateran Treaty of 1929 established formal relations between Italy and the Vatican. This is a strictly defined legal agreement between two governments intended to preserve the freedom of the church to teach and minister to the faithful.

Because of his work with the Italian government in formulating a concordat with the Vatican, Attorney Francesco Pacelli had access to Pope Pius XI. Eugenio congratulates his brother on this great accomplishment for the church. In many private letters to his brother, Eugenio expressed his desire to be removed from the nunciature. He wanted to be among the people and minister to them. He had no desire to be made a cardinal. This was a promotion the nuncio knew would be forthcoming. So he begs Francesco to mention his wishes to the pope. But to no avail.

On December 5, 1929, *L'Osservatore Romano* made the announcement. Pacelli received orders to report to Rome. He left Germany on December 12 in the midst of the tears of tens of thousands of German people who were lined up along the streets to the Anhalter railway station, following his car, holding banners, and lamenting his departure.

When Adolf Hitler was nominated chancellor of Germany on January 30, 1933, the first official step taken by the Vatican secretary of state, Cardinal Eugenio Pacelli, who six years later would become Pope Pius XII, was to defend the Jews. The Holy See sent documents informing the apostolic nuncio in Berlin to "officially represent the Vatican defense of the Jews with the German government and to alert the Nazis about the dangers of anti-Semitic politics." Throughout his life, Eugenio Pacelli was never anti-Semitic.

In a letter dated March 12, 1935, to Cardinal Schulte of Cologne, Cardinal Pacelli attacked the Nazis as "false prophets with the pride of Lucifer," labeling them "bearers of a new faith and a new gospel" who were attempting to create a "mendacious antinomy between faithfulness to the Church and to the Fatherland."

The following month, he delivered an address before a quarter of a million people at Lourdes, April 25–28, 1935, where he described the Nazis as "possessed by the superstition of race and blood" and declared that "the Church does not consent to form a compact with them at any price." Describing the speech, the *New York Times* headlined its story: "Nazis Warned at Lourdes" (April 29, 1935).

Cardinal Pacelli represented Pope Pius XI on many occasions. He was sent to Buenos Aires, Argentina, aboard the *Conte Grande* and presided as papal legate at the International Eucharistic Congress, October 10–14, 1934. He was also Pope Pius XI's delegate to France for the closing days of the Jubilee Year honoring the nineteenth centenary of Redemption. In 1936 he visited the United States of America.

Pacelli's first stop in America was St. Patrick's Cathedral in Manhattan and the residence of Cardinal Patrick Hayes. There he lunched with Nicholas Murray Butler, president of Columbia University. He visited the Empire State Building and admired the skyline of New York. Later, in Philadelphia, he saw the Liberty Bell. He made a whirlwind tour of the United States: Cleveland, Chicago, Notre Dame, San Francisco, Boulder Dam, Minneapolis, and Kansas City. At Fordham and Notre Dame University Pacelli received an honorary degree. He made contact with every aspect of American life.

On March 2, 1939, the world learned that there was a new pope. Cardinal Pacelli would now be known as Pius XII. But the next day in Germany, the Nazi newspaper *Berliner Morgenpost* stated: "The election of Cardinal Pacelli is not accepted with favor in Germany because he was always opposed to Nazism."

Sister Pascalina Lehnert, his housekeeper from 1923 to 1958, served him faithfully. In her memoirs[2] she explains that one day Pius XII prepared an official protest to be published the following day in *L'Osservatore Romano*. As he entered the kitchen and stood before the blazing fireplace, he told Sister Pascalina that he decided not to have his protest printed and would now burn it. She objected and reminded him that it might be useful in the future. Pius XII said: "This protest is stronger than that of the Dutch bishops. I thought about filing

---

2. Sister Pascalina Lehnert, *Ich durfte ihm dienen: Erinnerungen an Papst Pius XII* (1982).

it but, if the Nazis come and find it, what will happen to the Catholics and Jews in Germany? No, it is better to destroy this strong protest." With that, he threw it into the fire. Instead, he ordered Amleto Cicognani, apostolic delegate in Washington, DC, to have the text of the Dutch bishops' protest published and circulated in the United States. However, in her memoirs, *Ich durfte ihm dienen,* Sister Pascalina explicitly states that Eugenio Pacelli warned the Germans against Adolf Hitler in 1929, four years before the dictator came into power on January 30, 1933.

Some Important Facts

Pius XII and the Catholic Church protested and condemned the Nazi-Fascist ideologies and the cruelties toward the Jews. The Nazis were opposed to the election of Pope Pius XII because he was always opposed to Nazism. In no way did Pius XII sympathize with the Nazis, nor did he approve the genocide. Pius XII and Jewish communities in the United States feared that too much talk would have resulted in a worsening of the situation.

No one can claim that enough was done. To claim, however, that the pope and the church failed to do more or that they were indifferent or cowardly is a grave historical falsification.

In Nazi Germany active resistance meant immediate arrest, usually death. Sebastian Haffner, a young anti-Nazi jurist, emigrated to England for political reasons in 1938. His book *Resisting Hitler,* written in 1949, was discovered after his death in 1999. His testimony is about a martyr, Count Helmut von Moltke, hanged in Berlin in January 1945. Writing to a friend in England, von Moltke described the impossibility of resistance in wartime Germany: inability to communicate by telephone, post, or messenger; the danger of speaking openly even to trusted friends who might be arrested and tortured; the exhaustion of people whose energies were fully occupied with the ordinary tasks of day-to-day survival; nineteen guillotines executing an estimated fifty people daily, the relatives cowed into silence for fear of suffering the same fate.

The Catholic Church consistently assisted Jewish victims of Nazi anti-Semitism.

This is supported by news reports, testimonies at the Nuremberg trials, documents in foreign archives, and research of reputable Jewish, Catholic, and other historians.

Adolf Hitler despised Christianity and saw the Catholic Church as an opponent.

As Vatican secretary of state, Cardinal Pacelli sent sixty protests to Germany between 1933 and 1939. He did not have the power to make Hitler obey him. He signed the concordat with Germany in order to protect the German Catholics and the church. Hitler also signed this agreement on July 20, 1933, promising freedom of religion; five days later he abolished the Catholic Youth Movement and forbade the publication of Catholic newspapers and religious processions.

According to the Nazi theory, Christianity's roots in the Old Testament meant that whoever was against the Jews should also be against the Catholic Church.

To give an idea of what the Nazis thought of Catholics, Konrad Löw presents an SS report, which states: "It is indisputable that the Catholic Church in Germany is decisively opposed to the governmental policy of opposition to Hebrew power. As a consequence, it carries out work in support of Jews, helps them flee, uses all means to support them in daily life, and facilitates their illegitimate stay in the Reich. The people in charge of this task enjoy the full support of the episcopate and do not hesitate to take away from Germans, including German children, the little food they have, to give it to Jews" (Konrad Löw, *Die Schuld*, 2002).

Nazi propaganda constantly portrayed the German bishops and the pope as traitorous and shameless supporters of the "international Jewish conspiracy."

However, the Catholic Church recognizes the spiritual origins common to Christians and Jews. Documents now reflect the understanding of St. Paul that the church cannot forget "she received the revelation of the Old Testament through the people with whom God, in His inexpressible mercy, made the ancient covenant." There is a permanent sacred bond between the church and the Jewish people. The New Testament cannot be understood in depth unless in relation to the Hebrew Scriptures.

Catholics were warned that Nazism consisted of ideas that Catholics could not accept without denying their faith.

There is ample documentation to show that Catholic bishops condemned Nazi theories. This was why the Nazis persecuted Catholics as well as, if not as much as, Communists and Jews.

The Nazis required the blind, deaf, and physically or mentally handicapped to be sterilized and forbade marriages between Christians and Jews.

Throughout Germany, supplementary decrees to the Nuremberg Laws of September 15, 1935, canceled civic rights of Jews and abolished voting rights; Jewish civil servants were forced into retirement; Jewish professors, teachers, physicians, lawyers, and all Jewish state employees were dismissed.

In 1939 the Nazis began a program of "mercy killing," and, toward the end of 1941, Hitler put the "Final Solution" into effect. There was no need for the pope to excommunicate him. He was automatically excommunicated because of his actions.

In June 1940, Benito Mussolini joined Hitler in the war and implemented his anti-Semitic policy with regard to the discrimination against and persecution of Jews. This was accomplished through the Italian educational system and the media. News services in Italy were censored and reports about German atrocities were considered propaganda by the Italians.

The Holy See's diplomacy made it possible to save thousands of Jewish lives.

Reporter Michael Bobrow wrote: "As a Jew who served as a correspondent overseas, I know how highly Pope Pius XII is regarded by the Orthodox Jews of Israel. His Holiness knew that making noisy bombastic speeches in downtown Rome was not the effective way to save Jewish lives." According to historian Andrea Riccardi, the Holy See's option for the diplomatic path was "common to other neutral subjects, such as Switzerland and the Red Cross," and had as its objective "to help the persecuted and work toward peace negotiations." Another historian, Pietro Scoppola, said it is difficult to judge the situation by today's standards: "The Church did not condemn openly . . . and chose the most useful way to save hundreds of thousands of lives." For example, it was only with Vatican approval that Catholic priests and nuns could disregard the strict regulations regarding access by lay persons to cloistered areas of convents and monasteries. Furthermore, the pope explained in a letter to Bishop von Preysing that he must leave it to bishops with knowledge of the local situation to decide whether protests would do more harm than good.

Through his public discourses, his appeals to governments, and his secret diplomacy, Pope Pius XII was engaged more than any other individual in the effort to curb the war and rebuild the peace.

The Catholic Church rejects any discrimination against human beings or harassment of them because of their race, color, condition of life, or religion.

The church deplores hatred, persecutions, and displays of anti-Semitism. In fact, on November 14, 1942, the Administrative Board of the National Catholic Welfare Conference issued a statement: "We feel a deep sense of revulsion against the cruel indignities heaped upon the Jews.... We raise our voice in protest against despotic tyrants who have lost all sense of humanity by condemning thousands of innocent persons to death in subjugated countries as acts of reprisal, by placing thousands of innocent victims in concentration camps, and by permitting unnumbered persons to die of starvation."

On January 26, 1940, the *Jewish Advocate* in Boston reported: "The Vatican Radio this week broadcast an outspoken denunciation of German atrocities in Nazi [occupied] Poland, declaring they affronted the moral conscience of mankind." This broadcast confirmed the media reports about Nazi atrocities, previously dismissed as Allied propaganda.

Italians saved the lives of thousands of Jewish men, women, and children from 1943 to 1945.

Many anti-Nazi and anti-Fascist Italians who helped save the Jews were executed or deported to German concentration camps, where they died of starvation, disease, or hard labor. Others, during the Nazi occupation of Rome, were compassionate and had the courage to take risks to save them.

Compared to most European Jewish populations, most Italian Jews were spared the tragedy of the Holocaust.

After the war several prominent Jewish families came to America.

There were Nobel Prize winners: Emilio Segrè (1959), Salvatore Luria (1969), Franco Modigliani (1985). Other prominent Jews achieved important positions.[3]

Jewish and Italian communities have been interwoven for over a hundred years. The two groups constituted a significant percentage of the people coming to the United States during the great twentieth-century immigration period. In the United States, although religion has been a barrier, intermarriage between Americans of Jewish background and those of Italian descent has increased. Italian American Jews, despite their small numbers, have made an enormous impact on American life.

Pius XII was well-known and well-loved all around the world.

Jews considered the pope a friend of democracy and peace and an enemy of racism and totalitarianism.

Many times during the horrors that befell Europe after the rise of Nazism in 1933, Pius XII faced agonizing decisions in his position as supreme pastor of the Catholic Church. One role he was totally committed to carrying out was that of universal pastor, of kind and loving father to all victims. Guiding his actions was the determination to serve God and those whose lives he could reach. Chief among the goals he prayed for was peace.

---

3. Their stories are told by Primo Levi (*Survival in Auschwitz: The Drowned and the Saved,* 1959), Carlo Levi (*Christ Stopped at Eboli,* 1969), Giorgio Bassani (*The Garden of the Finzi-Contini,* 1970). Books and movies depict this traumatic period.

Thirty cardinals and bishops — from Italy, Spain, Portugal, Mexico, Japan, and the United States — who are members of the Congregation for the Causes of Saints voted unanimously on May 8, 2007, to recommend that Pope Benedict XVI formerly declare Pope Pius XII "Venerable."

Appendix

The Quest for Sanctity

Pius XII's *Last Will and Spiritual Testament* written May 15, 1956, in preparation for his death, is "must" reading for anyone interested in his spiritual journey. Two years later, following a brief illness while at his summer residence in Castelgandolfo, Pope Pius XII prepared for his eternal reward.

The *Last Will and Spiritual Testament* begins with the words: *Miserere mei Deus, secundum magnam misericordiam tuam.* (Have mercy on me God, according to your great mercy.) "These words which I, knowing myself to be unworthy of them or equal to them, pronounced when I accepted with trepidation my election to the supreme pontificate, I now repeat with much greater foundation at this time when the realization of the deficiencies, shortcomings and faults of so long a pontificate in an epoch so grave, brings my insufficiencies and unworthiness more clearly to my mind."

Pius XII states his sentiments with great clarity:

I humbly ask forgiveness of those whom I may have offended, harmed, or scandalized by my words and my actions.

I beg those to whom it pertains not to occupy themselves with or preoccupy themselves about erecting a monument to my memory. It will suffice that my poor mortal remains be simply deposited in a sacred place, the more obscure the more welcome.

I need not recommend myself to prayers for my soul. I know how numerous are these which the norms of the Apostolic See provide and the piety of the faithful offer for a deceased Pope.

Neither do I find need to leave a spiritual testament, as so many praiseworthy prelates normally do. The many acts and discourses decreed and pronounced by me because of my office, suffice to make my thoughts on various religious and moral questions known to anyone who might perhaps wish to know them.

Having set down this, I name as my universal heir the Holy Apostolic See from which I have received so much, as from a most loving Mother.

One notes that after acknowledging his shortcomings and faults, he asks forgiveness of those whom he may have offended, harmed, or scandalized by words and actions. He names as universal heir "the Holy Apostolic See from which I have received so much, as from a most loving Mother."

Eugenio Pacelli's purpose in life was to achieve sanctity. The total observance of both the theological and cardinal virtues is recorded among the thousands of testimonials and depositions prepared for his beatification by people who were in contact with him throughout his life.

As we approach the fiftieth anniversary of Pius XII's death, we must reexamine his actions and words during his lifetime and especially during his pontificate from 1939 to 1958. Did he truly practice the Christian virtues of faith, hope, and charity, as well as justice, prudence, temperance, fortitude, poverty, chastity, obedience, humility, and prayerfulness?

Pius XII was endowed with all the gifts of the Holy Spirit and, to a heroic degree, with all the virtues, theological and cardinal. He was a prayerful, serene, tranquil individual, dedicated to his every duty as pontiff. By his very nature, he was a meek and timid individual and preferred a quiet and serene atmosphere: sweetness versus severity, persuasion versus imposition. He was an orator and prepared himself conscientiously for each discourse. Then, without notes, he would improvise and abandon himself to his inspiration.

Very humble and truthful, he considered others equally so. As he frequently prepared his own documents, he would eliminate expressions he felt were too strong and insert more gentle phrases. He wanted everyone to be satisfied when they asked for favors, concessions, or dispensations and found it difficult to refuse the persistent demands of some people. However, during important discussions he was not timid and was always ready to respond clearly.

As pope he was known to ponder over his decisions and never obliged anyone to accept a nomination. He merely made it known that it would please him. In all his words and actions, he was guided by his love of God, his devotion to Our Lady, and his concept of the dignity of the Papacy. He protected the church and, for many years, diligently worked with learned churchmen to prepare for the Second Vatican Council.

For the love of God and of the countless people whom he touched with his compassion, Pius XII willingly accepted the interior "dark night of the soul." He remained faithful to his duties and supported all trials as he continued his intense prayer life. His trust in God enabled him to advance along the path to holiness despite the many trials and calumnies.

During the papal audiences, his faith, his hope, and his love for all were felt by millions of faithful who were inspired by his fatherly concern, his smiling face, and his inspiring words. Repeatedly he called on Our Lady, to whom he was especially devoted from childhood. He assured everyone of his prayers and embraced the whole world in imitation of Christ on the Cross, who, burdened with the iniquities of humanity, cried out, "My God, my God, why have you abandoned me?"

Early on, Pope Pius XI recognized the goodness and virtue of his secretary of state, Cardinal Eugenio Pacelli. He appreciated his keen intelligence and his capacity to radiate an interior peace and spiritual beauty. On several occasions he sent him to countries as papal representative and encouraged him to accept an invitation to make an "unofficial" visit the United States.

A few months after Pope Pius XII's death, a prayer with the *imprimatur* of Bishop Peter Canisius, vicar general of Vatican City, was circulated among the faithful:

O Jesus, eternal High Priest, who didst deign to raise Thy faithful servant, Pius XII, to the supreme dignity of Thy Vicar on earth and to grant him the grace to be a fearless defender of the faith, a valiant champion of justice and peace, zealous in proclaiming the glory of Thy most holy Mother, a shining example of charity and all virtues, deign now to grant us, in view of his merits, the graces we ask of Thee; so that, made certain of his efficacious intercession with Thee, we may one day see him raised to the honors of our altars, Amen.

Bibliography

Actes et documents du Saint Siège relatifs à la Seconde Guerre Mondiale. Edited by Pierre Blet, Robert A. Graham, Angelo Martini, and Burkhart Schneider. Vatican City: Libreria Editrice Vaticana, 1965–81, Tomes I–XI (Tome III in 2 vols.).

Bertone, Cardinal Tarcisio. *L'Etica del bene comune nella dottrina sociale della Chiesa.* Vatican City: Libreria Editrice Vaticana, 2007.

Blet, Pierre. *Pie XII et la Seconde Guerre Mondiale d'après les archives du Vatican.* Paris: Perrin, 1997. Trans. by Lawrence J. Johnson as *Pius XII and the Second World War: According to the Archives of the Vatican.* New York and Mahwah, NJ: Paulist Press, 1999.

———. "Controversy: Pius XII: Was There a Culpable Silence with Regard to the Holocaust?" *Inside the Vatican* (May 1998): 52–57.

Carroll, James. *Constantine's Sword: The Church and the Jews — A History.* Boston: Houghton Mifflin Co., 2001.

Carroll-Abbing, John Patrick. *But for the Grace of God.* Rome: O.N.C.R. and New York: Delacorte Press, 1965.

Chadwick, Owen. *Catholicism and History: The Opening of the Vatican Archives.* Cambridge: Cambridge University Press, 1978.

Cornwell, John. *Hitler's Pope: The Secret History of Pius XII.* New York: Viking, 1999.

Dalin, Rabbi David G. *The Myth of Hitler's Pope: How Pope Pius XII Rescued Jews from the Nazis.* Washington, DC: Regnery, 2005.

———, and Joseph Bottom, eds. *The Pius War.* Lanham, MD: Lexington Books, 2004. Bibliography by William Doino.

De Felice, Renzo. *Storia degli ebrei italiani sotto il fascismo.* Torino: Giulio Einaudi Editore, 1961.

Gilbert, Martin. *Auschwitz and the Allies.* New York: Holt and Company, 1981.

———. *The Holocaust: A History of the Jews of Europe during the Second World War.* New York: Holt, Rinehart and Winston, 1985.

———. *The Righteous: The Unsung Heroes of the Holocaust.* New York: Holt, Rinehart and Winston, 2003.

Goldhagen, Daniel J. *A Moral Reckoning: The Role of the Catholic Church in the Holocaust and Its Unfulfilled Duty of Repair.* New York: Alfred A. Knopf, 2002.

Graham, Robert A. *Vatican Diplomacy.* Princeton: Princeton University Press, 1959.

————. *The Vatican and Communism in World War II: What Really Happened?* San Francisco: Ignatius Press, 1996.

————, and David Alvarez. *Nothing Sacred: Nazi Espionage Against the Vatican, 1939–1945.* London: Frank Cass, 1997.

Jenkins, Philip. *The New Anti-Catholicism: The Last Acceptable Prejudice.* New York: Oxford University Press, 2003.

Kurzman, Dan. *A Special Mission: Hitler's Secret Plot to Seize the Vatican and Kidnap Pope Pius XII.* New York: Da Capo Press, 2007.

Lapide, Pinchas. *Three Popes and the Jews.* New York: Hawthorn Books, 1967.

Lapomarda, Vincent A. *The Jesuits and the Third Reich.* Lewiston, NY: Edwin Mellen Press, 1989.

Lehnert, Pascalina. *Ich durfte ihm dienen : Erinnerungen an Papst Pius XII.* Würzburg: J. W. Naumann, 1982.

Levai, Jenö. *Hungarian Jewry and the Papacy: Pius XII Was Not Silent.* London: Sands and Company, 1968.

Löw, Konrad. *Die Schuld* (The Guilt). Gräfelfing: Resch, 2002.

Marchione, Margherita. *Yours Is a Precious Witness: Memoirs of Jews and Catholics in Wartime Italy.* New York and Mahwah, NJ: Paulist Press, 1997.

————. *Pius XII: Architect for Peace.* New York and Mahwah, NJ: Paulist Press, 1999.

————. *The Fighting Nun: My Story,* New York and London: Cornwall Books, 2000.

————. *Consensus and Controversy: Defending Pope Pius XII.* New York and Mahwah, NJ: Paulist Press, 2002.

————. *Shepherd of Souls: A Pictorial Life of Pius XII.* New York and Mahwah, NJ: Paulist Press, 2002.

————. *Pope Pius XII.* Milan: Ancora Press, 2003.

————. *Crusade of Charity: Pius XII and POWs (1939–1945).* New York and Mahwah, NJ: Paulist Press, 2006.

————. *Did Pope Pius XII Help the Jews?* New York and Mahwah, NJ: Paulist Press, 2007.

Michaelis, Meir. *Mussolini and the Jews: German Italian Relations and the Jewish Question in Italy 1922–1945.* Oxford and Milan: Clarendon Press, 1978.

O'Carroll, Michael. *Pius XII: Greatness Dishonoured.* Dublin: Laetare Press, 1980.

Palazzini, Cardinal Pietro. *Il clero e l'occupazione di Roma.* Rome: Apes, 1995.

Rychlak, Ronald J. *Hitler, the War, and the Pope.* Huntington, IN: Our Sunday Visitor, 2000.

———. *Righteous Gentiles: How Pius XII and the Catholic Church Saved Half a Million Jews from the Nazis.* Dallas: Spence, 2005.

Schad, Martha. *Gottes mächtige Dienerin: Schwester Pascalina und Papst Pius XII* (God's powerful servant: Sister Pascalina and Pius XII). Munich: Herbig Verlag, 2007.

Tardini, Domenico. *Pio XII.* Libreria Editrice Vaticana, 1958.

Tornielli, Andrea. *Pio XII: Eugenio Pacelli un uomo sul trono di Pietro.* Milan: Mondadori, 2007.

Wolff, Walter. *Bad Times, Good People: A Holocaust Survivor Recounts His Life in Italy During WW II.* Long Beach, NY: Whittier Publications, 1999.

Zolli, Eugenio. *Before the Dawn.* New York: Sheed & Ward, 1954. Reprinted with the title, *Why I Became a Catholic.* New York: Roman Catholic Books, 1997.

Index

Numbers in **boldface** indicate photographs and portraits.